DESERTS

THE FIRST FIVE YEARS

OF THE WATERSTON

DESERT WRITING PRIZE

Published by:
Waterston Desert Writing Prize
P.O. Box 640
Bend, OR 97709
www.waterstondesertwritingprize.org

Cover photograph by Scott Nelson
ISBN: 978-0-578-52030-8

Printed in the United States of America.

Dedication

With sincere gratitude
to Dana Whitelaw,
Executive Director of the High Desert Museum,
for inspiration, leadership and collaboration.

Contents

Foreword by Rebecca Lawton   7

Foreword by Dana Whitelaw   8

Introduction by Ellen Waterston   9

2019

Winner   Nathaniel Brodie, *Borderlands*   10

Finalist   Summer Hess, *Terrae Incognitae Atacama*   20

Finalist   Michael Kula, *A Track Alone in the Sand*   28

2018

Winner   Patrick Mondaca, *This Cruel Land*   38

Finalist   Kathryn Wilder, *Getting Ready*   50

Finalist   Diana Woodcock, *Arabian Desert Revelations*   60

2017

Winner   Naseem Rakha, *Everything is Temporary*   70

Finalist   Kendra Atleework, *Sweetwater*   80

Finalist   Charles Hood, *Mono Lake*   92

Finalist   Lawrence Lenhart, *My Son Was Born to Rob Me of the Glory of Saving the Black-Footed Ferret*   98

2016

Winner   Tara FitzGerald, *No Water of Their Own*   106

Finalist   Kenneth Garcia, *The Hollow Places of the World*   116

Finalist   Kimberly Meyer, *Sewage Pilgramage*   132

2015

Winner   Rebecca Lawton, *The Sentinels*   142

Finalist   Nathaniel Brodie, *The River That Will Remain*   154

Finalist   Maya Kapoor, *Three Essays*   162

Finalist   Caroline Treadway, *Love and Botany—a Work in Progress*   176

Author biographies   184

Thank You Valued Donors   190

Board of Directors   192

Foreword

PLAYA and the Waterston Desert Writing Prize are a natural pairing, like great wine with an exquisite meal. The Waterston Prize builds bridges: from the first glimmer of creativity to a finished book, from the Great Basin to countless other ecosystems, from central Oregon's vibrant writing community to the world. Part of that bridging leads to PLAYA, because any writer winning the Waterston Prize also earns a stay at the PLAYA residency program for artists and scientists. It's part of the deal— and it's sweet.

At PLAYA, we are transforming the world through creative inquiry. We believe the planet needs voices elevated in celebration of arid places, which are under increasing pressure as our environment changes. The Waterston Prize selects excellent and diverse writers through a thoughtful selection process that complements PLAYA'S own. Here, prize winners sent to us via that process immerse not only in solitude and time but also in our mission: PLAYA nurtures innovative thinking in the arts and sciences. Every day, we strive to promote dialogue and positive change in the environment and the world. How fortunate PLAYA is to be partnered with a writing prize that honors artistic excellence, sensitivity to place, and desert literacy—with the desert as both subject and setting.

The Waterston Prize, like PLAYA, is a force for good at a time when writers face dark forces on the world stage. Right now, when words and research are called fake or are made to disappear, the PLAYA and the Waterston Prize offer another beautiful natural pairing: of people and place.

Rebecca Lawton
Executive Director
PLAYA

Foreword

Creating a place for dialogue begins with creating an experience that reminds people of their common values and vision. The High Desert Museum believes that there are core beliefs that enable all humans to connect. With that premise, we create experiences that remind us that we each value beauty, wonder, and a future that holds these values dear. The Waterston Desert Writing Prize is one of those experiences. The High Desert Museum is a proud collaborator and, with the Board of Directors of the Waterston Desert Writing Prize, joins in celebrating the fifth year of this important annual award that brings our attention to desert narratives worldwide.

Dana Whitelaw
Executive Director
High Desert Museum

Introduction

This commemorative anthology of writing is in happy celebration of the fifth anniversary of the Waterston Desert Writing Prize! Congratulations to all the winners and finalists of the past five years whose work makes up this fine collection. The Prize, started in 2015 thanks to an endowment fund started by actor Sam Waterston, and after whom the Prize is named, has grown in size in every way: number of annual submissions, number of attendees at the annual event, and the size of the Prize, starting at $1,000 five years ago to $2,500 in 2019. Also included is a four-week writing residency at PLAYA, an artists and scientists retreat located on Summer Lake. The annual awards ceremony, co-hosted by the High Desert Museum, is activities-packed with creative writing workshops, "A Desert Conversation" panel discussion anchored by noted authors, readings by finalists and the winner, and a festive reception.

That this prize has so quickly become coveted worldwide, if the geographic distribution of annual submissions is any indication, is thanks in large part to this innovative partnership with the High Desert Museum and PLAYA. On behalf of the Board of Directors, I sincerely thank them both for their belief in the importance of this literary award. Supporting writers who are engaging in literary exploration of deserts across the globe through art and science, metaphor and memoir, brings us all to an awareness of the importance of dry climes in the human narrative.

Most of all, the growing success of the Prize is thanks to the very hard work of the Board of Directors of this volunteer-run nonprofit. Their job description includes everything from affixing stamps to writing grants, from jurying the blind submissions to hosting guest authors at their homes each year. The Prize is also profoundly grateful to its donors— individuals, businesses, government agencies and foundations. 2019 was notable not just because it is the Waterston Desert Writing Prize's fifth birthday but also because it was the most robust fundraising year to date, making it possible to create the beautiful commemorative anthology. May you enjoy it as much as you enjoy this year's awards event.

In gratitude,
Ellen Waterston

2019 Winner

Nathaniel Brodie

PROJECT DESCRIPTION

In the past two decades seven jaguars (*Panthera onca*) have been treed, photographed, or physically captured in Arizona and New Mexico. The presence of large felines more commonly associated with tropical jungles in the deserts of the Southwest opens one to wonder and curiosity. The dogmatic finality of a thirty-foot high wall cutting an arbitrary border across hundreds of miles of the jaguar's desert habitat does not. The essays within *Borderlands* will weave together the stories of the Apache Wars, the current migrant crises, rewilding schemes, The Rosemonte Copper Mine, and the threatened freedom of movement of endangered species such as jaguar, ocelot, and Sonoran pronghorn.

Borderlands

THE TRACKS WERE PRESSED so perfectly in mud as to seem intentional, as though the cougar had chosen two strides to reveal itself. As though it were winking at me.

It was the first of May and I was counting the trees that winter had felled across a trail on the North Rim of the Grand Canyon. Later that week my crew would come back and cut the trail through the windfalls, but right then I had a whole day to walk an easy ten miles. The North Rim was still closed to tourists; little chance I'd encounter another human. I was happy to be alone.

The bright, high-altitude sun slanted through the spires of pines, and the first burst of wildflowers—wild candytuft, golden peavine, mariposa lily—burned through the darkest patches of forest. Thin drifts of snow remained in the north-facing drainages and deeper tree wells; the trail, still wet with snowmelt, was stamped with animal tracks: squirrel, coyote, turkey; their tracks glyphs of hunger, whim, instinct, territory. I'd stop from time to time and study the spoor, and so walking and stopping I came across a muddy divot displaying the lion's left forefoot and right hindfoot, the tracks about three inches long by three and a half wide.

I held my hand over them. As though they gave heat.

There is something special in coming across predator tracks—the lion residue not only preserved in mud but hanging in air, cuing some suddenly sensitive psycho-olfactory sense, exciting some long-dormant primal impulses. It is particularly pleasing coming across predator tracks on the Kaibab Plateau, the scene of one of the most storied predator-eradication campaigns in modern history.

IN 1906, TEDDY ROOSEVELT established the Grand Canyon Game Preserve, which encompassed much of the Kaibab Plateau. The logic behind a game preserve was simple—set aside a safe haven for game animals so that, free from human hunting, they could reproduce and repopulate other areas, thus ensuring a continual source of wildlife for hunting or tourist viewing. By that time, deforestation and unregulated hunting had severely reduced the populations of every major game species in the United States. Elk, once the most widespread of all North American ungulates, had been extirpated from the eastern United States. Bison, reputedly once the single most numerous species of any large mammal on earth, teetered on the brink of extinction. The endling passenger pigeon, the last of a species that had flown overhead in billion-bird flocks once estimated to be a mile wide by three hundred miles long, would soon die in captivity.

And yet, as the logic of the times dictated, protecting game animals in a game preserve necessitated not only the elimination of human hunters but also the elimination of natural predators. So between 1906 and 1923 federal government hunters on the Kaibab Plateau trapped, poisoned, and shot 781 mountain lions, 4,849 coyotes, 554 bobcats, the entire population of 30 wolves, and an unknown number of great horned owls, golden eagles, California condors, badgers, and foxes.

A century later no one knows how many cougars roam the Kaibab Plateau. The Forest Service, based on "harvest" information and observed lion sign, now estimates there to be roughly sixty to eighty cougars on the Kaibab Plateau, a population deemed "healthy and robust" enough to allow hunters to hound, tree, and casually shoot for sport a dozen cougars a year. Mountain lions have probably realized that the National Park's arbitrary boundary forms a safe haven—especially considering how heavily logged and extensively roaded the adjacent Forest Service lands are—and thus may not be accounted for in the Forest Service's "harvest" tallies. But according to the Park Service, "Research has not yet determined the exact number of lions [on the South Rim], nor has it concentrated on other areas of the park."

Thus it was a treat to come across cougar sign where they had been systematically slaughtered, to follow the tracks and find a pile of scat. I probed the shit with a stick: it was at least 90 percent fur. I continued walking, pleased to tread the same trail as a cougar had, to slide under the same deadfalls, to be harassed by the same Steller's jay. The trail switchbacked down a steep slope, crossed a sunlit meadow, and wound up in a thickly wooded draw. In the middle of the trail lay an object that my eyes, struggling to readjust to the darkness of the timber, could not quite recognize. A long moment passed before I recognized it as a deer leg.

Enough fur had been gnawed off to expose the still-articulated femur, tibia, and fibula. A tuft of fur remained where bone met hoof. Moving slowly uptrail, I found another leg, similarly ravaged, then the rest of the kill: the spinal column, the scattered ribs, the halved lower jaw. In a hollow off the side of the trail lay the antlers, a fine dichotomous pair still attached to a large portion of skull. I picked them up. Maggots burst like a broken pustule from the brain cavity.

I gagged, dropped the antlers, and looked around nervously. The drainage was choked with downed trees and hemmed by steep slopes rimmed by outcroppings of Kaibab limestone. Earlier in the day I had taken my knife out of my pocket and replaced it with my binoculars; now I took the knife back out of my pack. The rational part of my brain suspected that the cougar wasn't still around—the scat was days old, the kill well worked over. But it didn't require much imagination to envision the lion watching me from a dark hollow. The quick stab of fear I'd felt at the maggots was a primordial feeling, one of the root human feelings, a feeling now as rare as a cougar sighting. It was a fear that may have helped me if I'd actually come face-to-face with a cougar, an occasion for which I have fiercely longed.

I have no doubt that I have been in the presence of mountain lions, that they have seen me and that I'd have seen them if I had only looked in the right place at the right instant; if, rather than being "lost" in thought, I had been present in the way that fear makes me present; in the way it made me hike the rest of the trail with my head up, looking not at the ground or the façade of surrounding trees, but through the trees, into the shadows of the woods. There: a gnarled, anthropomorphic aspen snag. There: the flit and parabolic swoop of a jay. Here: the dry butterscotch scent of a yellow pine and the giving crunch of its litter underfoot.

The fear was more than a reminder to be attentive to the world: it served as a warning that our particular species of hominid is neither the center of this world nor ever apart from it; that, to a number of nonhuman animals, our brilliant, dominant species remains nothing more than meat.

THE INHERENT INDIFFERENCE and austere conditions of the Grand Canyon kept me humble, true, but not in as visceral a manner as the thought of a 130-pound cat bursting from a bush and crushing my windpipe. And not just cougar: in autumn, the South Rim's thousand-pound bull elk swell with testosterone to the point that they'll stand in the middle of the road and stare down passing RVs with bloodshot eyes and open mouths, almost hallucinating with anger. Once, at my trailer on the South Rim, I watched a rutting bull antler the absolute hell out of what looked to me like a rather unoffending metal trashcan. I was amused at the time, but biking back to my trailer that night I could hear the clack of antlers and moan of bulls battling in the roadside meadows and feared that in the dark an elk would mistake me for a charging rival.

And yet most of my animal encounters in the Canyon lacked that wild edge, the animals both boring and bored by acculturation. There was the old ram calmly chewing its cud in the middle of Bright Angel Trail, impatient crowds backed up on either side. There were the wild turkeys, gorged on Cheetos and territorial hormones, who attacked tourists and mule trains down at Phantom Ranch. The coyote gagging on road-killed carrion, the rattlesnake with its head crushed by a rock, the condors tagged like retail products. The time Michael felled a dead aspen whose rot-hollowed core hosted a squirrel's nest made of fiberglass insulation. The bushy-tailed woodrat who'd made a nest out of our mason twine.

But cougars, cougars cannot be made boring, or fat, or tainted by pre-vious contact. They cannot be controlled except by being killed. Which is, of course, why they are killed, and so, too, why I love them, and so want to see one, on its own terms. I may have seen one, once, in the Klamath Mountains of Oregon. I clattered around a dirt road bend in my jalopy and saw a tawny back end slink quickly into the downslope brush. So quickly it could, in fact, have not been a cougar at all, and despite what I swear were the distinctive scratching-at-the-road motions of a panicked feline, maybe only my desperate want made a cat out of an ungulate ass. Regardless, if it was a cougar, it was a split-second sight of a creature consumed by fear, not exactly what I have in mind when I long to fill, as

D. H. Lawrence put it, the "gap in the world, the missing white frost-face of that slim yellow mountain lion!"

And yet the potential cougar's fear was fitting. Both cougar and Canyon once embodied the sublime; both emanated power, silence, beauty; both induced awe, astonishment, and reverence as easily as they did the ecstasy of terror, horror, passion. Though both Canyon and cougar still retain these traits, their power, in a remarkably short time, has become debased, diminished. They have become capable of being overwhelmed; they have become overwhelmed.

THE GRAND CANYON IS an integral component of American mythology—a vast, titanic, and wholly unique landscape; a tabula rasa that embodies the dramatic natural and human histories of the West. I bought into that myth for awhile, bought the narrative the park sells so well: the Canyon's opened earth as unspoiled as the day the first human looked across it. Many of us did. When Ray, barely eighteen, came to work on Trails in the Canyon after a conservation corps summer in the Yosemite backcountry, he was thrown in with Michael—a wry Chicago realist—and Wayne—a libertarian Christian. Looking out across the great expanse of bared rock, Ray casually mentioned something about places like Yosemite or the Canyon being the real world, and everything outside of them as elaborately constructed fallacies.

"Bullshit," said Michael, without looking up from his work.

Ray stared at him, stunned.

"The world on the rim is the real world," said Michael.

"Yeah, the Canyon is the fucking bubble," I said.

"But, but—" Ray stammered.

"No. They're right," said Wayne, and so another debate began.

The Canyon, we reckoned, is inextricably bound to the surface world; it is permeated with humanity's historic and current presence. This permeation, this presence, has had, and still has, its effects, and not just with the effect of animals grown accustomed to humans. There's Glen Canyon Dam, releasing the silt-strained waters of the Colorado in accordance with Phoenix's use of air conditioners. There's air pollution: whereas at one time one could stand on the North Rim and look across seventy miles at individual trees on the San Francisco Peaks, the nearby

Navajo Generating Station has dispersed so much particulate matter over the region, that, along with natural dust and smog blown in from Los Angeles, and Phoenix, and, as recent evidence suggests, China, on most days the peaks were only a hazy pyramid. There's light pollution: while the Grand Canyon region is still one of the most and last starbright places on the continent, its night sky is increasingly washed out by the city lights of Phoenix, 220 miles away. So much other evidence of our inescapable presence: the roads and trails, the fire-suppressed forests, the mines contaminating the river, the helicopter-spewed fire retardant leaching off the rim to stain the fulvous Kaibab red, the fact that even much of the water emanating from the Canyon's springs is "hot" with tritium from decades of nearby nuclear weapons testing.

This is our world: where even in a national park the skein of our presence is laid as thick as the desert vegetation. A world in which nature no longer has a monopoly on the sublime. Where the Canyon is less relevant to our daily lives, less impressive, in a way, than what Leo Marx dubbed the "technological sublime": the dam plugging the Colorado, the knowledge that the weight of the impounded water behind such dams has shifted the way the world spins on its axis. The dominant catalyst for indescribable awe tinged by terror is neither Canyon nor cougar but the sheer quantity of pavement laid across the desert basin of Los Angeles.

This is far more terrifying than the fear of a cat in the woods. A cat I could flee from or fight. At least try. If I had encountered that lion that day in the woods, I like to think that my fear would have been instinctive, open, even enlightening. It would have been far less pernicious than my fears of the violence that humans so readily inflict upon other humans, and far more honest, even reassuring, than my intellectual fears of ocean acidification, or antibiotic-resistant "superbugs," or any of the other forms of slow violence we wreak on the world.

In The Thunder Tree: Lessons from an Urban Wildland, Robert Michael Pyle writes: "If we are to forge new links to the land, we must resist the extinction of experience." This comes in the context of his greater discussion about "the state of personal alienation from nature in which many people live," in which he argues that "we must save not only the wilderness but the vacant lots, the ditches as well as the canyonlands, and the woodlots along with the old growth."

The extinction of experience may be why I attempted to infiltrate that elk herd at the idiotic and wonderful age of sixteen: being raised in Los Angeles, I had never before been blessed with such an opportunity. The extinction of experience is why I left Los Angeles, seeking to live in the last places that offered such experiences. And yet even in these last places we encounter this lack, this negative feedback loop: I can't help but think that if we had more face-to-face experiences with cougars and wolves and grizzlies we might be less afraid of their presence—or future presence—in our midst.

Or maybe not. The renewal of experience could easily have the opposite effect, providing the old forms for our now-general fears to reinhabit. Numerous studies have shown that people—even the Inuit—are evolutionarily hardwired to fear snakes and spiders. This could certainly be true of lion and wolf as well. If the wolf's tooth "whittled so fine / the fleet limbs of the antelope," as Robinson Jeffers put it, it also shaped my mind to start at shadows and my hands to grasp for knives. Certainly more experiences with mountain lions would likely lead to more attacks on humans, and thus rekindle and renew the urge to exterminate and eradicate. If I may consider the occasional cougar attack a small price to pay for a more genuine and balanced coexistence, I'd obviously be rather upset if Erika were to be carried off and consumed by a large carnivore. From a distance, often an urban distance, it's easy to speak blithely of restitching our frayed relationships to the nonhuman world, to speak positively of abstractions like keystone predators and trophic cascades and ecological communities. Yet picking through the rent and rotting flesh of a deer carcass, it's far more difficult to ignore the potential for the sudden and striking peril that shadows these creatures.

But that's the point. Even if the fear persists, even as the fear persists, we can learn from it. Accepting fear is not about ignoring it, and certainly not about eradicating the external trigger, but about coming face to face with it by addressing the internal source: in this case our primal insecurities, the relict terrors of beasts beyond the reach of the cave's firelight. It is remarkable to consider how many of our current ecological calamities arose—and are sustained—not simply through ignorance or anthropocentric worldviews, but also through our attempts to overcome our ancestral fears. Likewise, it is interesting to consider the possibility that, as Gary Snyder posited, "ignorance and hostility toward wild nature set us up for objectifying and exploiting fellow humans." If this is true, we can gain some solace in the Jeffers line, "Old violence is not too old to beget new values"—it may be that by replacing these anachronistic fears and hostilities with new, ecologically based values and ethics, as well as humility, empathy, attentiveness, acceptance, courage, and discipline, future generations may still live with cougar and wolf and bear and elk. It may be that they will be kinder to one another.

I realize that most people would not embrace even the ecological violence of the cougar kill with the same edged joy I experienced that day. But I'm not entirely alone. After all, and somewhat ironically, the Grand Canyon Game Preserve, and the subsequent eradication of predators to protect game species, was created in large part because, as Daniel Justin Herman points out in *Hunting and the American Imagination,* upper- and middle-class New Englanders who considered themselves "sportsmen" were looking back "on the exploits of real men like Daniel Boone, and fictional hunter-heroes like Natty Bumppo, with a nostalgic longing to recapture for themselves the spirit of independent, self-reliant manhood they sadly lacked in their own urban, industrial lives." A century after these sportsmen decided to protect game animals by killing predators, I was following in their atavistic footsteps, longing for the old days when one could wander across the Kaibab Plateau and come face to face with wolves, bear, and cougar. I suspect that this longing impels the millions of people a year that visit national parks and wildlands; I know that Ray, Michael, and Wayne felt the same way, no matter what we felt constituted the "real world."

Those days may come again; I may yet have the chance to walk through a rewilded Kaibab Plateau. In October 2014—years after my encounter with the cougar kill—a female gray wolf was spotted on the Kaibab Plateau, having traveled at least 450 miles from her home in the northern Rocky Mountains. She was the first wolf on the plateau since the 1940s. Still, her visit may be a onetime occurrence: if the U.S. Fish and Wildlife Service—the modern-day iteration of the same agency that helped systematically exterminate wolves from the lower forty-eight states—removes Endangered Species Act protection for all wolves, there is little chance that wolves will be able to recolonize the areas they once roamed, even prime habitat like the Kaibab Plateau.

In his essay about the extinction of experience Pyle says, "We must become believers in the world." The world as it is: for human, for wolf, and for cougar. I agree with this, but it's difficult. Sad. I once heard a mule wrangler leading her tourist wards down the North Kaibab Trail say, "Teddy Roosevelt had to come and kill all the wolves and cougar on the North Rim because they were killing our deer." *Our* deer. Three months after the itinerant wolf graced the Kaibab Plateau, she was shot dead in Utah by a man intending to collect the $50 that Utah pays per coyote pelt. This is the world we must believe in. That day I found the cougar kill, I finished my hike at a parking lot crowded with Park Service law enforcement. They were mostly young white men, all uniformed, all with an undercurrent of aggression, a hint of provocation, emanating from the way they gathered around their vehicles. They had just finished firearm training, and the parking lot was littered with empty shell casings. I skirted through the woods to avoid them, feeling more vulnerable than I had all day. ⌇

2019 Finalist

Summer Hess

PROJECT DESCRIPTION

Gustavo le Paige de Walque was banished from his post as a Jesuit priest while serving in the Belgian Congo in 1952. Colonial administrators could not tolerate the rumors of unusual and illegitimate conversion practices, and the priest was reassigned to an even more isolated corner of the unraveling European empires: San Pedro de Atacama, a tiny Andean town in Chile's high desert. Le Paige continued to blur the lines between ethnographic research and evangelism in northern Chile. He traded much needed supplies for tours of local cemeteries and exhumed thousands of beautifully intact corpses. He crafted himself into the country's foremost anthropologist and founded its first academic journal in the emerging discipline of anthropology. He used the journal to support an ambitious but unsanctioned calling: to prove that the human race did not originate in Africa but in South America and that the Atacemeños were the true descendants of the original man. Le Paige is but one of many complex personalities that have collided in the fluid boundaries of the Atacama Desert. This project will cultivate a literary study of people and place by examining which narratives have been glorified and which have been subverted; what cults of personality and schemes for wealth have risen and fallen across historical time; and how we can support the remaining Atacemeños and their exploited landscapes.

Terrae Incognitae Atacama

"The most fascinating *terrae incognitae* of all are those that lie
within the hearts of men."
                    —John K. Wright, 1996 Presidential Address
                    of the Association of American Geographers

YOU CAN ONLY APPRECIATE the desert's power if you stay, if you
quiet your breath from a cavernous roar to a diminished whisper, and if
you complement rather than agitate the silence.

To stay does not mean that you live here. To live here implies a loyalty
that will never take hold of your erratic attention; it demands a fuller
engagement less consumed by comparison and translation. You will
never be able to live here. But you can stay. You can pause. You can sleep
700 nights under an endless revelation of stars and a front-row seat to
the cosmic forces of the universe expanding. You can tightly orbit the
brackish salt flats and voluminous volcanoes for 700 days.

You know right away, as everyone does, that San Pedro de Atacama is
a site of passage. A through place. A brief battleground for the Spanish
before moving on to more verdant territory. A petrol stop before the
mountain pass for trucks delivering goods from the Chilean ports to
Paraguay and Argentina. A quick three-day visit for tourists on a Chilean
holiday, according to guidebook consensus.

You begin to study a particular class of wanderer, a class that falls
away from the qualifiers "local" or "tourist." People with ancestral claims
to this land call them *afuerinos* or "people from away"—even though they
share the same nationality. They participate in the same national school
parade every Monday, where boys and girls of each grade line up by
height and hold steady like tiny soldiers as teachers inspect their school
uniform and send them home for minor infractions like dust on their

shoes. *Afuerinos* move to San Pedro as a statement against this military-style approach to order and control. They feel different here so far away from Santiago or any other major city. This oasis of thin rivers and dusky green trees is also an oasis of self-expression and experimentation. The town perches in the widest part of the country, two mountain ranges away from the coast that has shaped so much of Chile's history and identity. San Pedro is every day a white canvas where unwanted qualities are burned off by heat, rather than washed clean by water.

The *afuerinos* move here by choice. They are guides who manage herds of tourists and shuttle them to places with historical and made-up names. They are chefs who put on a show through culinary infusions, a category of food invented for destinations where the local fare could not be fed to clients with sophisticated palates. They are hostel owners, wait staff, and concierges who manage the total sensory immersion of tourists who pay to experience San Pedro.

You are friends with the *afuerinos*. They call you affectionate diminutives of your name. They touch your short girl hair and see the skin of your body. When not working in the art of illusion they thrive in the cult of golden-hour mysticism. They seek sunsets, hot springs, mountaintops, and hidden canyons. Some trip on drugs and others seek a more spiritually centered transformation. They are attracted by phenomena that live outside the containers of language. They are experts of diversion and see mystery—mystery as inexplicable beauty and not a problem to be solved through formal inquiry. They see mystery as potential.

You too feel something like worship, something like reverence, for what surrounds. Your temple is the high desert lakes that haunt the unsuspecting mind and occupy the consciousness of believers. There is a rational explanation for lakes: they are fed by subterranean springs or small creeks from snowmelt at higher elevations. But your mind still struggles with the calculation, thinks: it does not rain here, and yet—this.

At first, in total stillness, there is no lake, only the strange suspension of sun and clouds below. Then winds surge and chop brittle colors into pieces of foaming glass. At every shifting angle of sun, a new lake. At every passage of swelling or dissipating clouds, a new lake. At every wind-affected ripple, new. At every vantage point, from salt-encrusted bank to blunted tops of discharged volcanoes, change. At every breath, with every blink, difference. Lakes are mirrors where all the energy and desire that have ever arrested the heart are reflected. There is no escape from yourself. Gaze into the murmuring water, and be never sure of who is staring back.

THE DRY MOUTHS OF CRATERS expand in permanent, breathless yawns as we drive south. Erosion lines trace down volcanoes like rips in pleated skirts. My companions are a physical anthropologist—who measures teeth in skulls, who taught me to know the difference between shards of rock and bone (bone sticks to tongue)—and a visiting photographer. She had tried to drive herself the day before to a faraway lake in pursuit of the perfect panorama and nearly ripped apart her rental car on the unmaintained road that dissolves into a borderless swath of desert between Chile and Bolivia. I had offered to give her a ride because I was curious about what she had come so far to see.

About 50 kilometers south of our starting point in San Pedro, I notice a group of passengers who have left the climate-controlled confines of a dust-free van to stare up at mid-morning. A white logo indicates they are from a five-star hotel in San Pedro. I pull over because I have never seen a group in this part of the desert before, which is many kilometers away from any of the typical destinations. The group's guide wears a wide- brimmed synthetic sun hat and a cell phone strapped in a black case around his bicep. He explains that we are standing at the Tropic of Capricorn in Chile's Atacama Desert, a line that marks 23°26'16" south of the equator. A tall, scraggly pipe planted close to the road represents the most southern latitude at which the sun can strike from directly overhead. From the top of the single pipe, four arms point in 90-degree angles in four different directions over the heads of the passengers. No signs mark this turn off the highway. I wonder how the guide had known it was there.

He arranges the group of about ten passengers shoulder to shoulder in the slim shadow of the metal arm that points east toward the Andes. "Now," says the guide, "you take five steps forward and remain for fifteen seconds. Eyes closed. Say nothing." The passengers hesitate. The tall couple with aggressively pale skin glance from the sides of their eyes to see what other passengers do. "Come!" the guide urges. "Five steps."

Eventually the group shuffles forward like a flock of restless pigeons. Someone tries to make a comment, but the wind throws his words away. The guide orders the group to return to the line. He says his name is Mauricio, and I am not drawn to him. He is an *afuerino* but not yet skilled as a trader of stories and carefully-designed magic. His spell is sloppy and not compelling. Still, most of his passengers obediently nod, though a few look stranded in the middle of the desert, balanced on an invisible line.

They repeat the drill, this time taking five steps backwards to the south, waiting fifteen seconds, and again returning to the line. "Which direction was warmer?" the guide asks, his sunglasses beady and black, his arms behind his back clasping elbows, his legs slightly spread in the stance of a commander. Some point to the north and others to the south. "That's right," he says to those who tentatively raise a hand to the north. "It is always warmer in the north because there you are closer to the equator."

The reactions of his passengers rise in whispers. A short woman, who stands beside her very tall son, nods as if she had known this all along. Her son's eyelids droop, and his eyes seem windswept. Another man looks concerned. "Really?" he asks in English. He doesn't have the words to expand on his dismay.

The guide closes the activity by inviting his passengers to participate in a ritual. He explains the tradition of the *apacheta*, rocks stacked on top of each other to indicate a place of importance, a kind of prehistoric road sign, before countries and tropics. Chaotic arrangements of sharp bouquets surround us. If someone tried to follow these signs, they would fall down dizzy. A young man in cargo pants and boots builds his *apacheta* by stealing rocks from one that has fallen over beside him. Other passengers walk slowly away from the landmark to gather their materials: pyroclastic rocks ejected tens of thousands of years ago from the nearby but now mostly dormant volcanoes.

As the passengers continue with their assignment, I approach the guide. I'm not sure what I want from him, but I thank him for letting me listen in on the tour. He asks me where I'm from—always the first question in a town where ninety percent of the population is from away.

"Did you hear me talk about the Inca Trail?" he asks. He points to the painted metal pipe, and I see a tiny silver plaque that says *Camino Inca*, not *Tropic of Capricorn*, the words nearly invisible as sunlight sparks sharply off the metal. "This is not the real Inca Trail. The real one is that way," he says, pointing vaguely west. I see only the shimmering highway and wind-bullied piles of rocky sand.

"You know, there is no real difference between north and south?" he continues, confessing to the sham magic. "It's psychological. Some people sense the difference and others don't." He compares his nonsensical game to the experience of exploring another nearby touristic destination at significant altitude. "It's just like the geysers. Some people think they are going to get sick from the altitude, and they get sick. Others with heart conditions don't know about the altitude, and they run around in the thin air like little children." Then he sums up his guiding philosophy in a single phrase. "You only need one thing to enjoy San Pedro," he says. "Imagination."

SAN PEDRO WAS A TOWN of 2,500 people in the 1990s; more than 10,000 consider it home now, but the population swells and recedes constantly with tens of thousands of national and international tourists each day. In many ways San Pedro still feels like a very small town, much like a set in Universal Studios feels like a real city. Also much like a set, the town seems to be animated by people reading from scripts; but everyone inherits a slightly different script, and people improvise without warning. The result is the subversion of old stories and the reckless consummation and proliferation of the new. In this era originality, inventiveness, and deception intersect to create the shifting narrative of place. The town is always regenerating, is constantly born. The Atacama Desert you know is stolen through conversations with other travelers and variations of their knowledge and dreams. Their imaginations invented this space and continue to convince you of it.

American geographer Walter Lippman describes how this happens:

> We shall assume that what each man does is based not on
> direct and certain knowledge, but on pictures made by himself
> or given to him. If his atlas tells him that the world is flat he
> will not sail near what he believes to be the edge of our planet
> for fear of falling off. If his maps include a fountain of eternal
> youth, a Ponce de Leon will go in quest of it. If someone digs

up yellow dirt that looks like gold, he will for a time act exactly
as if he had found gold. The way in which the world is imagined determines at any particular moment what men will do.

He reminds you that you are here, then, to see what men will do, and
to work backward from there to capture their imaginations, or what they
dream.

You begin with the history of travel because it's written down and
holds still longer. It's easier to examine, like studying a glass of water
in your hand instead of an entire ocean. You learn that the first people
who wrote about the desert saw it as the last chance to provision before
continuing through the *gran despoblado,* or the great uninhabited or
uninhabitable expanse. The desert was vast, barren, empty, and a place to
be suffered through in order to arrive at greener, more fertile, and more
useful territory.

During the Spanish conqueror Pedro de Valdivia's first visit to San
Pedro de Atacama in the 16th century, he wrote of his intention to rest
there for nearly two months "in order to continue the journey and pass
through the great deserted space that was before us."

It was discoveries of nitrates in the 19th century that brought profi-
teers to the region. The Atacama Desert supplied the world with this
white gold—a resource that spurred the War of the Pacific and Chile's
land grab that annexed huge swaths of once dispensable, but now highly
coveted, desert from Peru and Bolivia. Even still, writers like Vicuña
Mackenna, a 19th century political writer and beloved chronicler of
Chile's history, found the region intolerable. For him, the desert was "a
country silenced by death. Without water, without vegetables, without
direction, without horizons...that region was the dark image of chaos."

This perspective gave foreign national companies full reign of the
desert for a hundred years and beyond. There were no demands for
regulation—at least from voices backed by economic power—and most
people welcomed any benefit that could be extracted from the useless
landscape. Industry had saved the land from bareness, and the region
was governed by a purely monetary ethic. Extraction had been nor-
malized and was unquestioned by the time copper, lithium, and other
minerals replaced the frantic mining of white gold, which halted after

the invention of synthetic nitrates in the early 20th century.

This language of desolation continues into the 21st century in the attitudes of scientific projects and new explorers. Project ALMA, the largest telescope array on the planet, released a book about patrimony in its high altitude site. It describes the region with echoes of generations and industries that have come before. "The area is located in one of the most desolate corners in the world, at 5,000 kilometers above sea level, where breathing is almost impossible. This remote corner of South America in the Central Andes is the home of ALMA."

You read these words and try to place yourself in the continuum of influence. You are here to witness, but also to mind Heisenberg. To see what is happening here, you have to understand your own disruptive forces. You begin by mapping the desert of your mind, an impossible task because at every moment the landscape shifts and light refracts.

The Atacama you see is a place of absolute tension so integrated into daily life that it is possible to forget this tension is real. You see the tension everywhere as symbol. It grows in the tight roots of the agarrobal tree and into full-grown pears the size of a baby's fist. The desert contains the quiet threat of *duende,* death ever possible, life a thread at best. It is the place where you have experienced the greatest range of emotion in the most compact amount of time. Dread tempered with company so it doesn't echo too deeply. Euphoria tempered with some semblance of a routine so that you don't slip.

This is how you know that when Jesus was lead by the spirit into the desert, he did not meet the devil. He gazed into a mirror and for the first time stared down his own fierce eyes. He was confronted by the sum of his potential and didn't recognize his selves. People had elevated him to the status of the Son of God, or a lunatic, or a liar, but in the desert he was none of these things, or he was all at once. Even the Son of God could not easily confront self, stripped down, alone.

And his disciples—they, too, have left their footprints, long swept away but still resounding. One in particular requires careful attention: Gustavo Le Paige, a Belgian priest banished from the Congo for irreverent evangelistic tactics, such as equating the Christ figure with local deities. He arrived in San Pedro de Atacama in 1952, nominated himself as the region's first anthropologist, and began to dig. ⌖

2019 Finalist

Michael Kula

PROJECT DESCRIPTION

A Track Alone in the Sand is a creative nonfiction account of the bicycle travels of Kazimierz Nowak across the deserts of Africa, as seen through environmental, historical, and cultural lenses. His travels lasted five years, from 1931 to 1936, and during this time, he took three thousand photographs, wrote a thousand letters home, and published hundreds of pages of essays in European periodicals. The perspective Nowak brought to the desert was remarkably sophisticated for its time: a perspective that might be described analogously as a combination of the environmental consciousness of Rachel Carson, the cultural sensitivity of James Agee, and the artful eye of Walker Evans. He remains, however, little known outside of his native Poland. I will complete fieldwork in northern Sudan along the Sahara/Nubian desert from Wadi Halfa southward, along a route mapped to coincide with places where Nowak wrote some of his most profound desert-focused writing.

A Track Alone in the Sand

Author's Note: This is a work of nonfiction. While select liberties have been taken with details to enrich scenes, the people, places, events, and descriptions are accurate representations of the facts of Kazimierz Nowak's experiences. Likewise, in places where the narrative captures the inner thoughts of the character, these too are based on observations and insights gathered from Nowak's writing and research. All passages in quotes, whether indicating dialogue or thought, are faithful translations of Nowak's own words.

Chapter One: Departure

KAZIMIERZ WAS TIRED OF WAITING.

Back in Poland, he had waited months—years actually—to be able to even attempt this journey. Selling photos for five zloty apiece until he'd saved enough for the rail fare to get here.

Then, last week when it was finally time to leave, he'd been forced to wait three hours in the station in Poznan on account of a delayed train. After that, there were several wasted hours more at the transfer station in Katowice, where around him he sensed the onlookers regarding him as a "circus monkey of sorts," on account of his disheveled appearance and his absurdly heavily loaded bicycle, which he wouldn't dare let out of his sight.

Then, there were more transfers. Vienna. Venice.

Waiting and more waiting, all of it without him having been able to "afford even one glass of something warm" to help pass the hours in the November-cold of those open-air stations.

And now finally, here in Rome, it had been more of the same. Waiting in the rainy street for a kind priest to have mercy on him and offer him lodging for the night and safe storage for his gear. Waiting for some cursed official at the consulate to discuss visas. Waiting for some tourist to fish a few lira from his pocket to pay for a photo postcard he'd taken of them in front of the Colosseum or Trevi Fountain.

It had been relentless—all that waiting—and now after four wasted days idling in the city, Kazimierz had enough. Africa was waiting. So, forgive him if he didn't feel full reverence for this moment; forgive him if he didn't pray along silently with the others there where he sat in the drafty hallway of the Vatican; forgive him if all he could think about were his empty pockets and his full bladder.

It was Tuesday, November 10, 1931, and for the past two hours, along with a dozen other pilgrims, Kazimierz had been waiting for Pope Pius XI to arrive. Father Felix, the kind priest who'd taken him in at the Resurrectionist church just off the Spanish Steps, had arranged this audience, suggesting subtly that perhaps if the Holy Father learned of Kazimierz's plans, the church might extend him charity and support for his journey. Or if not that, then at the very least the pope's blessing might help ensure his safety with all that might lie ahead.

This wasn't Kazimierz's first time here in the reception rooms of the papal household. In fact, it was to be the fourth private audience he'd had during his life: the first, when he was just a boy—fourteen—with Pope Pius X, when Kazimierz had come here impulsively by train from Stryj without even telling his family; the next, after the Great War, with Benedict XV, when Kazimierz passed through the city as a newly freed soldier; and the last, four years ago with Pius XI, the same man for whom he was now waiting, when Kazimierz had first attempted and failed at this almost comically-ambitious plan to cross the continent of Africa alone by bicycle. The pope's blessing apparently hadn't helped him last time, so Kazimierz's hopes today were instead fixed mostly on the faint prospect of receiving some tangible gift of support from the church, something that would, if not fill his empty pockets, then at least let him finally put an end to all this waiting. He needed one hundred and twenty "stupid lira" to be exact. Roughly ninety dollars in today's equivalent. With that, he could pay for his visa and his ferry ticket, and finally be on his way to Tripoli and beyond.

At last, the heavy door at the end of the hall opened. Kazimierz settled himself, sitting up straight on the bench. One of the priests who'd been supervising the visitors during this two hour delay instructed several of the women to remove their gloves and cover their shoulders. Then the priest told them all to kneel on the marble floor, which Kazimierz did with great deliberateness, given the discomfort caused by the pressure of his belt on his full bladder.

A moment later, a pair of Swiss Guards entered the hall in their mustard-and-blue renaissance uniforms and took their places on each side of the doorway. Two cardinals appeared immediately thereafter. And then behind them, as Kazimierz recognized even from far, was Pope Pius XI. He was dressed in a white cassock, and aside from the brightness of his red shoes and the glimmering immensity of the jeweled cross around his neck, he appeared unadorned. His face from that distance—plump and full despite being in his seventies—seemed to have barely changed since Kazimierz's last visit. Wire spectacles gave him the air of a physician or professor.

As the cardinals began moving toward the group, Kazimierz turned his gaze toward the floor in humility. The marble beneath his knees felt cold, and his neck, stiff for so many days with the chilly rain, ached from the penitent angle of his head.

Eventually the rustling sound of the men's vestments drew close and white shoes moved into view where Kazimierz stared at the floor.

"*Sei Tedesco?*" a voice asked in Italian. "Are you German?"

Kazimierz looked up, his eyes immediately meeting the expectant face of a silver-haired cardinal.

"No," he said. "*Polacco,*" he said, and then waited, thinking his clear competency in Italian would encourage another question from the man. Perhaps about his home parish? About his time in the city? About the purpose of his visit? Something that could ignite small conversation and offer him the opportunity to explain his grand plan, to respectfully share his financial hardships, though certainly not ask directly for any charity.

The cardinal, however, only nodded in response and seemed content to move on.

Kazimierz then shared his name. "Kazimierz Nowak," he said. A last-ditch effort to stir conversation.

But there was nothing. The cardinal simply nodded again, made the sign of the cross over Kazimierz's head, and moved forward toward the elderly couple kneeling beside him in the row.

And then, there he was. The Pope. In front of him. His hand outstretched inviting Kazimierz to kiss his ring, which Kazimierz did,
noting how warm and fragrant the man's hand seemed. This, he would be
certain to tell his wife Mary later in the letter he would write home to her
about this day. She would like hearing that detail.

Then, as Kazimierz let go of the pope's hand and raised his gaze,
he felt himself grow flushed as their eyes met for a momentary
connection. To his surprise, the pope's expression was more sullen
than he might have guessed. Warm and welcoming, yes; but at the
same time, his eyes appeared almost cloudy, which Kazimierz read as a
look of "despondence." Perhaps something grave had caused his delay
today? It was hardly an uncommon expression to see on people's faces
nowadays—what with the wretched state of affairs in the world right
then—but it was still startling to see it here, especially on the face of
the Holy Father, and seeing it, Kazimierz understood immediately that
there would be no miraculous offering of support from the church,
no generous handout to sponsor his journey. No. He would have to
be content with a blessing, which the pope then promptly gave him,
crossing Kazimierz on his forehead as he whispered over him in Latin.
At the completion of this, Kazimierz crossed himself, lowered his head,
and watched as the pope moved forward to the next pilgrims, repeating
the same encounter with each one until he reached the end of their
line, where he turned and immediately "walked back along the other
side of the hallway, disappearing with his entourage" through another
set of doors.

Just like that, the visit was over, if one could even call it a visit,
hardly worth the long wait it didn't seem, and the chaperoning priests
immediately ushered Kazimierz and the rest of the group from the hall.
Together they moved down a flight of stairs, past another pair of Swiss
Guards standing sentry beside a massive set of double doors, and then
out into the gray, rain-shined cobblestones of Rome, where despite the
chill in the air, Kazimierz's first thought surely had been one of relief.
He didn't need to wait any longer. If nothing else, at least now he could
finally relieve himself.

❖

IT IS EASY TO FEEL SMALL IN ROME. You feel it in the shadow of the Colosseum, marveling at how such a building could have been constructed nearly twenty centuries ago and how it has stood for so long. You feel it in the open air of the Pantheon, staring up at the oculus and the full hemisphere of its dome, lost for perspective in the immensity of its vacuous space. And you feel it in places like the Sistine Chapel and standing in front of works like Bernini's *Apollo and Daphne*, which may not dwarf you with their physical size, but surely do with their imaginative power and their near-unfathomable artistic perfection.

And then of course there's time. History. The way the city seems to have existed forever and will continue forever, hence the nickname the Eternal City, or, *Wiecznego Miasta,* in Kazimierz's own words home to his wife. Standing on a bridge over the surreal blue-green of the Tiber, it is easy to let the magnitude of the place, both its physicality and its enduring identity, overwhelm you and make you feel like you and your life are an insignificant speck in both space and time. Standing there though, it is also easy to let the place sweep you in the opposite direction, if you allow it, and make you feel as though you are something greater than you are, to feel as though you are an integral piece of some cosmic puzzle and, as such, you are called to strive for a greatness worthy of that place.

It's no surprise to me then that perhaps more than any other city—certainly more than any other outside of Poland—Kazimierz Nowak loved Rome, since his was a life that seemed to teeter on this edge between despairing insignificance and grandiose ambition, a sentiment, I suspect, that could just as easily be applied to the existential identity of his beloved homeland of Poland. It is also no surprise to me then that during that cold and wet November of 1931, during those last days he would ever find himself in the city, Kazimierz sought comfort in the small places of Rome as he waited. Aside from that one visit to the Vatican, Kazimierz did not seek out the grand tourist destinations any longer than needed to make a few lira from selling photos. And he did not attend his daily masses in any of the seven pilgrim churches, but rather in the small chapel with the Resurrectionists downstairs where he was lodging or a few blocks away at Sant'Andrea delle Fratte, where he could sit in the shadow of Bernini's "Angel with the Crown of Thorns," virtually alone, except for a handful of nuns and other locals from that Quirinal neighborhood. Indeed, even though he wrote Mary telling her how much he wanted to show her "the marvels" of the city, Kazimierz only "left the monastery when necessary," taking comfort most of the time in his "modest monastery cell...with its whitewashed walls and black cross, the bed, desk, and cabinet, the windows with the view of St. Peter's, and the green garden below." Perhaps it was the simplicity of it that helped buffer any anxieties he felt about what was to come, as his mind raced ahead to dreams about pedaling across the great Sahara or alongside the Nile or Zambezi. No matter the reason, he was content to live "like a monk," he said. Once, after a week of living there like this, he even wrote to Mary saying that "The monastic life had its appeal." And "when you live it," he said, "your soul is at peace, and you can even find happiness."

Even find happiness. Kazimierz wrote this apparently without recognizing the irony or the insult his words might hold for her: Mary, his wife, whom he'd left to care for their children as he went off for another of his adventures. Because, of course, Kazimierz wasn't a monk. He was a married man. Nine years now. And he was a father of two: Elzbieta, nine, and Romuald, six. And he was an out-of-work bank clerk who professed that this trip was to help his family, not to get away from them, so perhaps what he meant with those words to Mary—*even find happiness*—was that he was pleased to find it—happiness—in spite of, not because of, his isolation and separation from them.

Riding the Kalahari

BY THE TIME WE REACH ARU, a game lodge on the edge of the Kalahari Desert in eastern Namibia, the sun is low on the horizon, a neon orange against the red, iron-rich sands of the surrounding terrain, and it's difficult not to recall all those Disney-like images of the African sun setting on the savannah. The cliché of the moment is made worse by the arrival of the lodge's attendant, who meets us in his truck at the gate in order to escort our painfully underpowered rental car through the lodge's vast property. The man is gray-haired and sun-baked, looking exactly the way you would expect for a man who spends his days working as a Professional Hunter in Africa, a government-certified profession here in Namibia. He appears the platonic ideal of a tough-guy.

From his truck, the man leans out the window and surveys our car with an incredulous expression, his eyes seeming to ask: you really drove here in *that*?

After a moment, he explains that we've come to the wrong gate. We missed the turn a half-hour ago; yes, the property is that big.

"It's about fifteen minutes ahead to the lodge," he says, nodding toward the road, which looks to be simply two ruts beaten in the sand. Then he gives a quick set of directions and gestures for us to pull ahead of him. "You go first. I'll follow. Just in case. But if I flash my lights, stop. You've gone the wrong way."

"Got it. Wouldn't want to get lost out here," my friend James says to him. A swarm of insects have gathered quickly outside. He swats them away, rolls up his window, and turns to me. "That guy looked like he was straight out of Central Casting," he says.

I nod in agreement. Like Crocodile Dundee, I think, but stop myself before I can say it, realizing that that's a cliché from a different continent.

James then hits the accelerator, harder than I'm expecting, and immediately we're skidding on the sand, a sensation that feels remarkably close to that of my car hydroplaning on the rainy highway back home in Tacoma. I can't imagine bicycling on this, I think, as I grip the arm rest.

"How fast are you going?" I say.

"Fast enough to impress *him*," James says, making a point to glance in the rearview mirror at the truck behind us.

I don't respond. It's a funny thing for him to say. Though at the same time I completely understand. It's hard not to feel triggered for some Hollywood-esque sense of heightened virility here. Not when you're face to face with a guy like that. Not when you're in a desert like this, in a-tin-can-of-a-rental-car that must weigh half as much as the two Black Rhinos we've been warned live on the property. And especially not when you're two middle-aged guys away from their families who've spent the past three weeks traveling a thousand miles across southern Africa. At every stop we've been cautioned about some new danger or another: leopards in the Western Cape; spitting cobras and black mambas in the

Cederberg; hyenas in the Namib; scorpions everywhere. So far, though, all those warnings have begun to seem like bluster. I haven't felt anything close to the fear everyone seems to want to ignite in me. But now, here, something suddenly seems different, and it's not just my friend's needlessly reckless driving.

This is my first time on the Kalahari, and compared to the Namib Desert, where we've spent the last few nights sleeping under a star-filled sky surrounded by undulating dunes that feel as soft as memory-foam against your backside, everything here on first impression seems so much harder, sharper. All around us there are spikey camelthorn trees reaching up from the ground like arthritic hands. On the sides of the road, still-dormant desert thistle bushes appear like clumps of rusted barbed wire. And all the while, insects pelt the windshield so forcefully that if it weren't for the smear of their crushed bodies on the glass, I would easily believe those sounds were from the impact of stones.

⁓

I HAVE NOT COME TO ARU to shoot anything, nor, for that matter, even to shoot at anything, which is clearly a novelty to the lodge's workers and the hunters we meet in the half-bar, half-lobby when we arrive. For my friend James, this stop is a bit of well-earned luxury, as he would surely describe it, amid the otherwise Spartan vacation he's made for himself by accompanying me on this stretch of my travels; but for me, this stop is research. I'm retracing a portion of the route of Kazimierz Nowak, a Polish journalist and photographer who bicycled across Africa in the 1930s, and here, less than three miles away from where I'm standing, at an old homestead that has since been absorbed into the vast landholdings of this opulent hunting resort carved from the Kalahari, he stayed for three weeks in the spring of 1934.

This place, for Nowak, was a monumental stop in his journey for two reasons. First, it was the longest he had ever stayed in one place during his five years on the road; and second, it was the place where he'd finally had to give up his beloved bicycle, which by then had taken an obvious beating during the nine thousand miles of travel that had brought him here. It was, by that time, a barely functional means of transport, with improvised spokes in the front wheel after the rim had been bent into a figure-eight near Cape Town.

That's why I'm here right now. That bicycle. I've corresponded with the lodge owners in advance, and while they basically laughed at my dream that there might still be some remnant of the bike here on the property, I have hope. In fact, last night on Namib, I dreamt of rusted handlebars sticking up from the red sand. You never know. ☜

2018 Winner

Patrick Mondaca

ORIGINAL PROPOSAL/DESCRIPTION

Editor's Note: Patrick Mondaca originally submitted a proposal for a book titled Adjustment Disorder. The following writing sample, titled This Cruel Land, is a chapter of the proposed book-in-progress.

What is it within the veteran that makes us so intent on killing ourselves? Do we simply have disdain for ourselves after coming home? It is a difficult thing, to try and answer these questions, and to comprehend all the why's.

I came back from Iraq and was discharged from the Army fourteen years ago, but it's only as of recent that I've really been making my way back—"back to the world" as Vietnam vets like to say. And I am just now beginning to feel as if I've almost arrived home again.

My way back has been long, longer than most, though some of us never do find our way. I think for years I didn't really want to come back. The Army gave me a sense of belonging and purpose that I lacked in civilian life. And I didn't find those things again until I went to the desert landscapes of Sudan.

My plan to continue the work of this memoir in progress is to go to an artist's residence in Morocco at the edge of Erg Chebbi, one of the largest sand dunes in the Sahara and live among the Berber people. Because I already have several chapters near completion, this fellowship will allow me to bring the book to completion in the North African desert environment I will be writing about.

The stories throughout this memoir thread together many perspectives: the lingering influence of religion in my life; the contemplation of life and death within the theater of war; the difficulties of transitioning back to a civilized peacetime society; and the discovery of personal peace in a desert landscape like Sudan by a combat veteran. The memoir seeks to advance desert literacy by drawing attention to the concept of the "draw" or pull of the desert in the postwar lives of military veterans such as myself, T.E. Lawrence, and Wilfred Thesiger.

This Cruel Land

"No man can live this life and emerge unchanged. He will carry, however faint, the imprint of the desert, the brand which marks the nomad; and he will have within him the yearning to return, weak or insistent according to his nature. For this cruel land can cast a spell which no temperate clime can match."

—Wilfred Thesiger

MY WORK AS A HUMANITARIAN began on a whim. I had been home for a couple of years after the coming home from the war in Iraq, going about the business of trying to adjust to civilian life. I finished a bachelor's degree in political science from a state college and stumbled through the motions of suburbia and family and policing. Finding this was all a bit mind-numbing, I fixated on anything that would offer me an escape. And in the spring of 2007, with *Save Darfur* signs and *Not on our Watch* posters on the front lawns of random houses and churches in town, I had an epiphany: I would go to Darfur. Even though I had never before given the crisis there much thought and I couldn't point to it on a map if my life depended on it, it was the best getaway plan I could come up with.

Having spent the majority of my adult life in military or civilian policing and with my only hobbies at the time being marathon drinking or taking long, aimless rides on my motorcycle, I was not the typical candidate for an evangelical humanitarian organization to hire as a field security officer in Sudan. And all I would have to do was babysit a few Bible-thumpers doing their penance. How hard could that be? I had run convoys through Baghdad for Christ's sake. It was brilliant. So, when the international staffing recruiter asked me to come down for an interview, I bought a suit off a Macy's rack and drove the fifteen hours through rainstorm and traffic over the Appalachians to see what fate might await me.

"Will you pray with me?" asked the woman in charge of my interview. *Oh hell no, lady.* I wasn't expecting that. I really didn't want to. I imagined my creator who was most certainly laughing at the scene unfolding far below. Well played, Jesus. The prodigal son, returned to the fold— on bended knee with folded hands and eyes closed tight. If only the fundamentalists back home could see me now. Humbled. Religion is a funny thing, isn't it? It kills and it saves; it condemns and it crucifies; it judges not, and yet it judges more than anything else. We despise it and run away from it, yet somehow it seems to suck us back into its grip. And there I was, having run far and long, and on the verge of running farther—deep in the heartland of American evangelicalism, after so many years, back on bended knee.

I tried desperately to remember how to pray and hoped she didn't expect me to follow her lead. I wanted this job, and I was intent on getting it—intent on getting out of the country even if I had to pray like the Reverend Billy Graham himself at a summer revival meeting.

"Um...sure," I stammered. "But, honestly, I'm a little bit out of practice and I'm not sure exactly what to say. It's been a little while...since...I said any..." My voice trailed off, and she put her hand over mine from across the table, closed her eyes, and started talking to God. About me. She was sitting across from me—holding my hand and praying for me and thanking God for bringing me to their doorstep. I found myself sneaking a peek at her face. She was so sincerely caught up in the moment, and I found it oddly calming.

I wondered if I should ask her, why they wanted to send an ex-soldier, far more heathen than believer, to help God watch over their people in Sudan? And why was there no one else chosen for this particular assignment? Was there none among them like Peter willing to pick up the sword in the garden of Gethsemane? But I never asked. Instead I signed a contract to go live and work in Darfur for a year. I caught a KLM flight out of Bradley International to Schiphol in September 2008. From Amsterdam I flew to Cairo, and then Cairo to Khartoum. And then from Khartoum to Nyala, South Darfur.

When I landed in Nyala, the sun was just cresting over the drab, dust colored little buildings. Stepping off into the cool early North African air, I listened to a familiar sound—the Adhan—the Muslim call to prayer, its long wail, rising and falling; God or Allah, his Prophet, welcoming me back to the desert. I watched a little warily as the box marked Dynamite tumbled onto the carrousel and made lazy circles through the baggage area in Nyala's small airport, and a hundred sets of hands, arms, and elbows jostled and shook it as they lunged for the steady stream of random cartons, boxes, sacks, suitcases and duffle bags that were being unloaded from the Toyota pickup trucks transferring the luggage from the tarmac. Crates of produce, bundles of printer cartridges, computer monitors, hygiene products, toys, and other consumer goods were being unloaded from the belly of the plane. Amongst the explosives and fruit and vegetables, I spotted and grabbed my unmistakably American military-grade, tan, hard-plastic foot-locker and moved quickly outside in the event that the place happened to go up in a plume of smoke along with everything else surrounding the baggage area. Stepping out of the air conditioning into a solid wall of dry 110-degree heat, I looked into the drab landscape and suppressed a small smile. Here I am then, back for more fun in the sun.

THE EVENINGS WERE THE ONLY TIME I could be alone to think and to write down my reflections on the day's happenings. Lying in a tent listening to the loose sidewalls flapping in the cool desert breeze, I stared up through the torn ceiling at countless stars clustered against a pitch-black sky. The only other time I remember seeing so many stars was in the Kuwaiti desert on the Iraq border. Lighting up a Benson & Hedges cigarette, I watched the smoke dissipate into the breeze, and tightened up the scarf around my neck. Outside of my tent, I savored the smell of the stew of tomatoes, onions, haricot beans, and sheep liver simmering over the open flame. Fresh pita bread picked up at the local souk was piled in a heap on a dilapidated plastic table.

My mind wandered back to the day's travels, and my body ached from the many hours of bouncing around in the old rented Land Rover. Ever so briefly, I wondered if I should be back home in Connecticut, grilling hamburgers out in the driveway with a beer. The flurry of meetings with Government of Sudan military, militia leaders, sheiks, and

UNAMID officers had become a blur—a never-ending rotation of small dingy glasses of super sugary brown tea, negotiations, backslapping and schmoozing. "This is the life in Darfur," my colleagues would say with wry smiles. The monotone of the prayers brought me back to the present. *What solitude—under a canopy of a billion stars in the middle of nowhere*, I thought. Giving the food a stir, I waited for the final mutterings of the prostrate men on their prayer mats with my notebook dimly illuminated by the orange glow of the cooking coals.

Mealtimes in Darfur were not for the conversational. In a place with such food shortages, meat was a luxury, and the guys on my team were happy to have it. In minutes, our pile of bread would disappear, be replenished, and then disappear again just as fast. Chunks of bread would be scooped into the savory stew and the biggest pieces of meat and fat greedily captured and swallowed quickly from the stainless-steel bowl. Steaming glasses of dark, sugary tea would follow the meal, along with a few raucous hours of dominoes, before the last of the men would call it a night. The occasional braying donkey and barking dog would be the only thing I would be able to hear above the snores coming from the neighboring huts.

This night, instead of waking up to the cool morning air and the symphony of donkeys, goats, sheep, chickens, roosters, and babies crying, I was abruptly shaken from my slumber by the tukle door being kicked open and the shadow of a man standing over my bed brandishing a dagger. Half-blinded from the flashlight I had instinctively flicked on, he rummaged through the tukle ripping my satellite phone out of its solar charging socket and slicing it from its cable. Snatching the keys to our trucks and momentarily appeased, the thief joined his comrades on the looting spree taking place throughout the camp.

Sanusi, the young camp manager, signaled silently that he wanted to make a break for the Sudanese military outpost and rouse the sleeping soldiers. If he were caught by our attackers, they would probably beat him, but they might also shoot him. I shook my head *no*, but Sanusi had already half-jumped and half-fallen over the perimeter fence and was in a full-on barefoot sprint.

I have often wondered what Sanusi was thinking in that moment. Young Sanusi, barely twenty years old—with just a hint of an early beard on his face—sprinting in the dark past armed bandits who wouldn't hesitate to shoot him dead. Arms and legs flailing, the soles of his feet cut up by the sharp brambles and rocks scattered along the path to the army checkpoint, he ran because all our lives depended on it. He was just a kid really, scrambling in the dark directly towards a Sudanese army or police patrol who wouldn't hesitate to shoot him if they were in a mood. Was he afraid? Afraid or not, he didn't hesitate. He just ran for it, returning with a platoon of soldiers who stood guard as we packed up the camp, and we were gone by sunrise. Two days later the village erupted and one of our neighboring NGO'S staff members was shot dead outside their compound.

IT WAS OVEN-HOT ALREADY and only 9:30 in the morning. Not quite yet Baghdad hot, where the dried sweat from the previous day's patrol molded your uniform into a dank crusted shell and your rubber boot soles stuck to the pavement if you stood in one spot for too long, but it was hot enough to make you think about it for a few seconds. The thing about being exposed to this kind of heat for any extended time is that you eventually forget how hot it really is. Some might say that your body becomes acclimated to it or that your mind simply stops registering the fact that it is draining pints of fluids by the hour. This is, of course, dependent on whether one has access to water, which I did, but thousands did not. How the people of Darfur survive even the natural forces against them is a remarkable testament to the human spirit and its will to live.

The two checkpoints between Nyala and Bulbul were manned by Popular Defense Force soldiers armed with small arms, generally Kalashnikov or Heckler and Koch G-3 assault rifles, wearing forest green uniforms like Government of Sudan forces. They would ask for cigarettes, sometimes water, never money. There seemed to be a standing order that these checkpoints were not permitted to collect the "road tax" from humanitarians. Though I imagine such collections were still occurring with commercial vehicles, lorries hauling goods and passengers where a soldier could easily bring in 20 to 30 SDG per passenger lorry if they were to tax each passenger.

I had learned to keep a few extra packs of Bensons on my dashboard simply to give out to checkpoint guards and national security officers. Having stood many military and police checkpoints myself, I knew first-hand how I had felt about the occupants of vehicles who would drop off cold waters in the summers and hot coffees and donuts in the winter months. I tended to be friendlier to those types, and we all did. These guys in Sudan were no different. Cigarettes and cookies seemed to work well enough, but when things were getting serious, the fastest way to the good side of a Sudanese national security officer was as simple as a Coca Cola and a Snickers bar.

A shot fired into the air got our attention. The soldier motioned for us to slow down and pull into the checkpoint. He wanted to chat so I stepped out of the vehicle and offered him a cigarette. A few words were exchanged but the only ones I said were the obligatory *Alhamdulillahs* a half dozen or so times. The soldiers liked that. Listening to the *Khawaja* attempting to speak Arabic made their day.

We halted the trucks in the village of Dogi to confirm our location and ask one of the locals to point out the best road to Umm Al-Qura. I had old coordinates from the UN Field Atlas plugged into my handheld GPS but these were unconfirmed, and I wanted to be certain before we went any further. Dogi, just across the wadi from where Umm Al-Qura was reported to be, seemed to be an extension of the Arab militia encampment purported to be there as several young men in various stages of military uniform were seen throughout the village.

Handing out cigarettes, the Bensons & Hedges gold pack favored by most of the locals throughout South Darfur, our driver Hassabo spoke with a couple men stacking long sacks of charcoal who pointed us towards the track leading to the camp. As we crossed the wadi, I noted the tactical advantage the militiamen would have over any would be attackers coming from this direction. A natural barrier of deep sand during the dry season and soft mud when conditions were wet, coupled with a high growth of reeds providing cover on the adjacent banks, the wadi would slow any advance from the east, and without air support, anyone stuck in between would be mowed down like fish in a barrel.

I could see, in the distance, several additional armed men and vehicles on a hill overlooking the track we were now on at about 200 meters. Assuming this was the checkpoint, Hassabo eased the lumbering Land

Cruiser forward, and focusing on the group of men and guns in the distance, the two of us failed to see the two men partially concealed in the reeds bordering the dirt track to our immediate left.

The crack of a 7.62mm round from a light machine gun fired over the roof of our truck broke the relative silence, bringing us to focus on the two young men now leveling their gun barrels at our faces. "Whoa!" I shouted. Almost swallowing his cigarette, Hassabo buried the brake pedal and the big Toyota ground to a shuddering gravel-grinding halt. We put our hands in the air. "Goddamn it," I muttered under my breath. *This just might be the end,* I thought. *What a weird way to go,* barely managing to keep these musings to myself.

One of the men approached us carrying a Chinese or Russian sniper rifle with a mounted scope. He was barely in his teens I guessed, the wild haired young Arab wearing desert camouflage pants, a worn brown t-shirt, and black leather boots. Boots, I had noted, were a rarity amongst fighters in South Darfur. Sudan Liberation Army rebels and even many Government of Sudan soldiers and police almost always wore sandals.

Recognizing us as unarmed humanitarians, the young man waived us on in the direction of the checkpoint on the crest of a small hill where I could now count a dozen or so well-armed men gathered around two pickup trucks outfitted with 12.7mm Doshka heavy machine guns. At the foot of the hill, another fighter armed with a HK-G3 assault rifle inspected our vehicles while a second individual manned a light machine gun position covering our every move. To the immediate right of this position, I made a mental note of the large caliber recoilless anti-tank rifle aimed down ominously over the track south to the wadi area.

The militiamen and vehicles bristled with daggers, swords, pistols, Kalashnikov AK-47 and HK-G3 assault rifles, sniper rifles with scopes, HAWN mortar delivery systems, RPG shoulder fired grenade launchers, light machine guns with bipods, heavy mounted machine guns, and anti-tank weapons. The men's faces covered in camouflage *shemaghs*, bodies attired in various desert or olive drab colored military uniforms, strapped into load bearing vests, bandoliers stuffed with cartridge magazines, belts of machine gun ammunition wrapped around waists and draped over shoulders, and intricate leather pouches containing bits of the Koran strung from every neck, bicep, waist belt, and bandoleer of every fighter to ward off incoming bullets.

It is a strange feeling the moment when you realize that if someone wanted to kill you, that they just could. And there wouldn't be anything you or anyone else could do about it. That one minute you could be a living, breathing person, and the next a crumpled, steaming pile of carrion rotting in the sun with small animals and birds carrying away your flesh to feed their young—circle of life and whatnot. In such moments, you look for something to remind you that you're still breathing: Blue sky. The warmth of the sun on your face. The fine dust of the desert landscape making your eyes run. Anything.

A slight man jumped down from the back of one of the Land Cruiser pickup trucks parked in the shade of the scrub on the hill. Wearing desert camouflage shirt and uniform trousers over bright blue track pants, as was the fashion, the man carried a bandolier of hand grenades, a dagger and pistol in his belt and an AK-47 rifle in his hands. Through Haroun's translation, he introduced himself as the area commander and instructed us to follow his vehicle to the schoolhouse where we would have our meeting.

In two pickup trucks, the commander and his two squads of fighters led us into the Umm Al-Qura interior. At a third checkpoint partially concealed within a small wadi manned by a team of fighters, I observed another pickup truck concealed in the tree line and on its truck bed was mounted a recoilless anti-tank rifle covering this smaller wadi's path south. These men appeared to have been in this position for some time as they were drying laundry on bushes. However long they'd been in this position seemed not to affect their vigilance as one fighter kept his RPG trained on my vehicle the whole time. When we pulled away, the fighter with the RPG gave me a friendly wave as if to say, *no hard feelings...just doing my job here, friend.* As if a few seconds before, he wasn't prepared to vaporize us where we sat buckled into our seats and go about the rest of his day. I waved back with a stupid grin on my face, happy not to be dead.

The meeting with the area commander would take place at Umm Al-Qura's school. Set apart from what appeared to be the training grounds, the school area had its own enclosed perimeter with two completed steel framed classrooms enclosed with a thatched material. Two smaller tukles housed a squad of militia and the other a schoolteacher. Across part of the yard was a volleyball net, and just outside, were two field latrines which were really just holes dug into the ground with a concrete slab over them featuring cut-outs over the open hole enclosed by shredded blue plastic tarp.

On metal folding chairs, Haroun and I took seats across from the area commander and we were introduced to the school's headmaster. An aid brought a tray with four bottles of water on it into the class-room although the headmaster offered to send for Pepsi if we preferred. Haroun and I accepted the water while silently wondering about the ges-ture. We rarely saw native Darfuris with bottled water unless they worked for an NGO. But the militiamen were not lacking for much it seemed.

TO DEMONSTRATE THE SECURITY of the roads and the patrol capabilities of his men, the area commander suggested we take a drive, escorted by his men, to the market at Sarma, a village just south of Umm Al-Qura. During the short trip, the militiamen maintained fairly decent convoy discipline. With one vehicle on point, its machine gun forward, my vehicle at the center, and a second vehicle bringing up the rear with its machine gun covering our flank, their patrol style was almost stan-dard operating procedure.

When Haroun and Hassabo stepped away for their afternoon prayers, I walked through the market purchasing some tomatoes, onions, pow-dered red pepper, salt, and biscuits to supplement our evening meal, and engaging the locals in my limited Arabic. The militiamen, while aware of the foreigner among them, seemed minimally interested in interfering with my stroll. When I returned to the vehicles, I accepted a glass of hot chai from one of the men who had escorted my team from Umm Al-Qura. Another young fighter asked me somewhat shyly for a *cigarette Amerki,* and so I passed around the reserve pack of Lucky Strike Silvers that I had been rationing. The fighters politely gagged on the bitter cigarettes until I was finished with my own but Bensons, they said, were better.

In Umm Al-Qura, the school headmaster invited my team to stay the night in an empty classroom. The schoolyard also housed a squad of armed fighters in various stages of militia attire who would also spend the night.

The following morning was a cold one. The fighters on guard through-out the night had gone and their replacements now huddled in the sliver of sunlight that was beginning to warm the crest of the hill. Long WWII era woolen overcoats now served to shield the lean bodies of the young men acclimated to the deserts of Darfur and Chad. In the distance, I could hear the shouts of men and the engines of vehicles cranking to life, gears grinding and exhausts backfiring in the cold morning air.

As we turned the trucks around and headed back east from the school to the small wadi checkpoint towards home, I watched as several groups of men conducted marching exercises and calisthenics in the training area. We passed through the checkpoints and headed northwest on the track to Jebra and Mershing leaving Umm Al-Qura behind us. Umm Al-Qura would no longer be categorized in our minds as merely a village, but as a military installation home to some of the most dangerous and well-armed men in Darfur.

Arriving back at the office in Nyala, I dropped my gear on my desk and grabbed a cold bottle of water out of the mini fridge we had splurged for in our office. Salah and Daud, our logistics assistants, were holding down the fort, "Welcome, brother. How was it?" Salah asked. As I recounted the story of the shot fired by the militiamen over the vehicle, the two young men from Darfur shook their heads empathetically making "tsk" sounds. Salah, who had long since begun applying the "f-word" to every possible use of his English vocabulary, said, "F-ing militias." "F-ing militias," I said. "F-ing Darfur," said Salah. "F-ing Darfur," said Daud. "F-ing Darfur," I said. *Alhamdulillah,* we all said together. And then we laughed because this was just "the life in Darfur."

Looking back on it now, wretched heat and mostly bad food, late nights and early mornings, long hours and low wages, there was no other place I'd have rather been or work I'd rather have done, both then and now. Amid the chaos, I was at peace. And I have missed it ever since. ᵥ

2018 Finalist

Kathryn Wilder

PROJECT DESCRIPTION

These Seasons of Disappointment: Cows in the Desert is a work of literary nonfiction that is part memoir, part science, and part literature of place. This project will address ranching practices in the desert West from an aging woman's experience and perspective as she questions the marriage of cattle and desert. Research will take place on the desert lands of the Colorado Plateau, where I run a heritage breed of cattle. While gathering data through close observation of the impact my cows have on the range, I will also observe other Colorado Plateau ranching outfits. For baseline comparisons I will visit cattle-free zones within Colorado Plateau public lands, such as Mesa Verde, Canyonlands, and Arches national parks. Fieldwork will involve daily ventures on foot and horseback, noting range conditions and asking: How are the salt-desert shrublands, the piñon-juniper woodlands, the riparian areas, and the Mancos Shale soil base handling the impact of this desert-adapted breed of cattle? How are the cattle handling the terrain? And: Should we be here at all? The ethical concerns of cows in the desert create an urgency that requires answers, thus inspiring the research necessary for completion of this project as I continue to monitor the health of our cowherd and rangeland. Since the dime novels of the late 1800s, the desert West has been a favorite setting for stories, yet little has been told from a literary perspective that combines a ranching lifestyle with environmental science. This book will do that.

Though often used in literature to represent a barren spirit, deserts are rich in life and story. Mine is a story in search of solutions, addressing important environmental considerations while offering an intimate look at cows as characters and the desert as home.

Getting Ready

It's already started, I think, as I tell the dogs to stay *right there,* holding
my hand up, flat of the palm to them, a stop sign. Both border collies
settle beside a bony stalk of greasewood and my attention returns to the
bull. He thinks he's hidden behind a bushy piñon pine, which in fact he
almost is, both tree and bovine squat and thick, but he's a Red Angus and
his color shows through the verdure like redrock, only here the sandstone is Dakota—pale pink—so he's darker.

I'm afoot, not ahorseback, and step slowly along the fenceline, making my way to the wire gate in the corner, glancing back at the dogs and
reminding them with my hand to *stay,* hoping the bull also stays put. His
choices: make a run down the fenceline, away; or down into the creek
bottom, away; or directly at the fence, over it or through it; or directly at
me.

I've been bumped by bulls before. It's not all that fun. One time I
was thrown over a fence by a younger version of this guy, a trimmer yet
equally powerful Red Angus bull whose head hit my butt and lifted me up
to the top rail of a six-foot fence, which I rolled over like a pole-vaulter,
smacking packed earth on the other side. My husband bending over me
to see if I was all right, I gasped for breath, impact and laughter colliding
as I managed, "I got a splinter," and held up my hand, the tip of a finger
smarting.

Now in my sixties, I'm more conscious of risk. In this remote valley, if
this bull were to charge and hit me, I might lie on the ground for a long
time before anyone bent over me, though surely the dogs would eventually stop staying and come to see what I found so interesting there in the
dirt. Each thing I do out here, from hoisting bales of hay, to stringing
barbed wire, to chasing off a neighbor's bull, has a shadow side of danger.
It's as if my physical vulnerability reflects that of the land—mistakes can
have long-lasting impacts.

I shouldn't be thinking these thoughts; I should pay attention. Bulls in general are temperamental, unpredictable. Moody, cowboys would say, as if bulls were women. Bulls are only with their cows a few short months each year, which might explain their easy turn toward anger.

I know my own bulls, their ages, genetics, and behaviors. Their names. And still, they're unpredictable. This bull I don't know, though I can guess he's not used to a woman angling around him on foot. Or talking to him.

"See the gate? Just wait where you are and you'll be out soon enough," and he watches me, his belly swollen with creekwater and the hay he tore loose from my stack while I was gone, the haystack now a mess.

It's not just the mess that irks me—it's the cost of time and hay and whatever other feed the bull has consumed. Yet technically it's my fault that he's here. In the fence-out state of Colorado, it is the landowner's responsibility to keep the fences up if you don't want other people's livestock on your property. Which I don't—I'm saving the feed for my own cows. While the Bureau of Land Management land surrounding me shoulders other ranchers' cattle and is sometimes grazed down to dirt, this inholding has cover, and winter feed. Which is probably what first drew the bull. Then he found the hay.

Most of this neighbor's cattle have already drifted down from the high country, and the cowboy, Jeff, who seasons at his ranch's headquarters thirty miles away, has been heading out ahorseback to gather the remnants. Each time I see him drive by with dogs in the truckbed and a horse in his trailer, I feel the pang of envy. I want to go, too.

In the ranch country of California, where I lived with my first husband, women were valued as near-equals when working cattle. Wives cowboyed with their husbands, the couple and their dogs able to accomplish most or all of the ranch work until it came to branding season, a favorite time of year when neighbors gathered together to brand hundreds of calves, women there in the corral right beside the men, roping calves, flanking, castrating.

"It's not up to me," cowboy Jeff has said when I've offered help, which means his boss has the final say, though I suspect it also means that Jeff is honoring the traditions of this part of the West. Of the ranch women I've met, some may ride with their husbands but few of them rope. That's a man's job. If women venture into the branding pen, they're handed syringes—vaccinating calves a task that requires minimal strength and skill.

Yet here I am, alone, afoot, dealing with Jeff's boss's bull.

Were I ahorseback, I'd be quicker. And taller. Safer. But the horses won't come out until Sunday, when we haul our cows to winter range. I will not wait until Sunday to kick this guy off my pasture.

Emboldened by my annoyance about the gender discrepancies that have followed ranching this far into the twenty-first century, I march to the corner, open the wire gate, drape it over greasewood instead of tucking it carefully out of the way, and walk back around behind the bull. The dogs haven't moved, nor has the bull, though now he sees the hole and steps out from behind his tree and through the gate onto the public lands that surround this quarter section of private. His tracks in the soft, dry Mancos Shale soil are inches wide and at least an inch deep, each of his steps a bigger impact on the land than any of the steps my cows will take.

"And don't you come back," I tell him.

Environmentalism, like gender equality, has been slow to make its way into contemporary ranching in the Southwest. This land is *tender*. If not well managed, it could deplete to nothing but dust. For my son Ken and me, running cows out here is an experiment. We have small cows, averaging 900 pounds, whereas the other cattle in this country are heavy English breeds, mostly Black Angus, and Red, like the bull. They weigh in at 1,200–1,300 pounds—the bull pushing 2,000—and have that much more impact than our small cows. Our question, though, is this: Does our breed justify us running cows—of any kind—in the desert?

It does justify my annoyance when the neighbors' cattle trespass onto my feed.

And yet, the trespass bull is my fault: my fence. As he waddles off, I close the gate and walk along the fence in the opposite direction, dogs at my heels. Approaching the creek, we push through dry, rattling coyote willows and some tamarisk that dares, like the bull, to invade the land on my side of the fence. Crossing the creek, shallow this time of year, I find a single set of wide, bullish, one-way tracks at a low spot in the barbed wire. The bull hulked over, nosed out the hay, knew where water was, and made himself quite at home.

Back in the circle of cell service that exists near a corner of my cabin, I text Ken: *Bull's out. Going to fix fence but it will look like a girl did it.*

I drink water and gather supplies. Hiking with the dogs back down to the place in need of reinforcement, in gloved hands I carry post pounder, T-posts, and a wreath of barbed wire, fence pliers and clips in my pockets. Using the post pounder and my weight, I force a T-post into the hardened accumulation of silt from the summer's biggest flashflood.

The clang of metal on metal pierces the morning air and bounces off the cliff face. Who hears it besides the dogs, the bull, and me? Mountain lion, bear, bobcat, mule deer? Cottontails, packrats, field mice? A pair of ravens drifts past. I stop pounding to listen to the whoosh of their wings pushing air. Ravens, the dogs, the disappearing bull, and I are the only creatures I know share this moment. I savor the sense of unseen possibility as quiet returns.

I only have a moment in which to relish the wild sanctity of this corner of desert—there is work to be done. Attaching a strand of wire to the T-post, I pull the wire body tight (I didn't bring the fence stretcher—not enough room in my hands), stringing it to another T-post, wrapping the wire around as tightly as I can and clipping it in place. Barbs poke at my gloves and snag the sleeves of my sweatshirt.

As I work I wonder why I felt the need to denigrate myself to my son. An echo of the internal conversation I've been having? The repair does not look "like a girl did it," though it may look as if a grandmother in her sixties did. If I didn't do it, and waited for a man's help, the bull would be back, gorging himself on my winter hay supply. I have to handle each thing as it comes: trespass bull, fence repair, highwater, frozen water. The animal in the night that stole a rubber dog-food bowl off the porch. Cutting, splitting, and stacking wood. Stacking hay.

It has begun, I think again: *winter.* Although it's really still fall, the last of the golden cottonwood leaves clinging to their branches, resisting the change in the season (like me), my time in the valley to watch cows for the winter has started.

Fence fixed, fencing tools returned to their stations, I sit briefly on the cabin porch, enjoying the noon sunshine and the dogs crowding my knees. The work was not hard but the day hasn't yet ended—I have to hook up the trailer, unload more hay, adding to the stack mauled by the bull, and drive eighty miles to town for additional supplies.

The raven pair swoops in, calling as they ride the updraft off the cliff face and float down to perch on a ledge of Dakota Sandstone. One raven struts along the edge as the other hops down a step to investigate something—perhaps spring's nesting site, to which they return each year.

Disappointment Valley runs generally east-west, from Colorado almost to Utah, sloping down in the east from the independent peak, Lone Cone, 12,613 feet tall, and in the south from the long Glade Mountain. The western end of the valley abuts redrock layers typical of southeastern Utah: Navajo Sandstone topping the Kayenta Formation, Wingate cliffs below. Our ranch comprises several non-contiguous parcels in this valley: our easternmost rangeland pasture, named for the family ranch that spanned five generations; the quarter-section inholding four miles to the west, where I live; and another piece another twenty miles west. Eighty miles away, the ranch headquarters near the small town of Dolores houses Ken, his wife, two children, and sometimes Tyler, my second son, along with dogs, cats, chickens, Navajo-Churro sheep, horses, and Criollo cattle. Our bulls and finishing steers will stay at the headquarters with Ken while the cow part of the cattle operation winters in this valley with me. My duties will primarily include breaking ice and feeding, as needed; counting cows; and, come spring, calving them out. Which means I watch the cows do the work, help if necessary, rare in our breed, and log the results.

In addition to the cows and dogs, two horses will be my winter companions. And, at least temporarily, there is one bull in the neighborhood.

Other than the bull, my immediate neighbors consist of a couple five miles east, the husband of which is the fourth generation of his family to ranch in the valley, and my friend TJ, who lives seven miles west. With my arrival, the valley started getting crowded.

A chill comes over me and I realize that beneath my sweatshirt the sweat of modest labor has cooled despite sunshine. It's time to either go inside to get warm or press on into the next task. I groan at the thought of hooking up the trailer, which is silly as it's not hard: I just back the truck under the gooseneck hitch, and when I'm lined up perfectly I get out and crank her down. It's the "perfectly" part that's problematic when alone—the ball must sit directly beneath the hitch, which sometimes means I get in and out of the truck half a dozen times to line it up right.

It would save time if another person were here to direct me, as well as stress on a knee that holds stories of earlier hardships—like getting thrown over a fence by a bull. I was young then and fearless, stupid, or optimistic, which might all be the same thing—the result of believing my body indomitable, pain or injury not in my foreseeable future. Now sometimes after a day like this, the knee gets so stiff and sore that needed sleep does not come for a long time. So I don't welcome the other job that awaits—unloading the hay—dropping the sixty-five pound bales then lifting them with back and knees up onto the stack.

And yet I chose this. I choose it every day.

It's not all a struggle. Riding is not hard, the horse, not me, bearing my weight. Getting the bull out was actually easy. Just a job to get done.

Other days the work is harder. Last week, on our hands and knees and then on our bellies like soldiers, Ken and I pushed through a stand of Gambel oak to get to the other side. Casually lumped into the scrub-oak category, Gambel oak is spread liberally around the Four Corners region. It grows thick there where we needed to work—on the south side of the canyon, which is the north face, where years of detritus hold moisture. The opposing sides smelled as different as they felt, one side dry, exposed sandstone showing geologic age and wear and harboring the sun's warmth, the side we were attempting to ascend pungent, shed leaves and twigs mixing with dark earth that smelled fertile, like soil not stone or dust.

It was truly one step forward, three back as my feet slipped constantly downhill, oak branches snagging my braid. Pushing a circle of barbed wire in front of me, with a free hand I clung to roots that held tightly to their own struggles. When Ken reached firm footing ahead of me, he grabbed the wire from above as I held on, and pulled me up to relatively solid ground, though the angles of our ankles remained precarious. The bucket with fence pliers, clips, and staples, and the rusting cans I find everywhere, slipped, tipping to its side as it rolled, and I had to slide back down to retrieve those supplies and claw my way back up.

So it went as we strung and tightened wire along the heavy metal T-posts graciously left by an earlier fence-builder. After that stretch of fence was complete, we stashed our tools and explored. At the rim, a large chunk of Dakota Sandstone, eroded at its base by water, wind, and time, made a protective overhang, and traces of black that was not desert varnish curled up the underbelly of the rock like smoke. Which perhaps it once was—stains left by early campfires, possibly of the First People who populated this land for eons before Spanish explorers came through, followed by sheepherders and cattle ranchers and bad guys like Butch and Sundance.

Yes, here in our valley, this cross-section of human backstory. And now us, and our desert-adapted cows, a heritage breed descended from cattle brought alongside horses and sheep by the explorers who sailed across the sea on Columbus's second voyage, in 1493.

On our butts Ken and I slid back down the steep, moist side of the canyon, clutching tools and bucket, me conscious of my knee, then crawled beneath the tangle of Gambel oak to creekside where we could stand and stretch and see again the high-desert sky.

WHILE MUCH OF THE WEST IS DESERT, this valley is high desert—upwards of 6,500 feet at the eastern end, 5,500 near Utah. It's hot in summer, usually more than 100 degrees in the valley during the month of June, and cold in winter, the first freeze coming in October, sometimes as early as September, the hovering-around-zero nights and into-the-teens days beginning in late November. December usually bears the coldest days. Sometimes in February we can wear T-shirts.

None of this is predictable. Not anymore.

Except June.

It's almost safe to say that June is the hottest, driest month in these parts. Years of weather records show this, not just my limited experience—although I have lived in each of the Four Corners' states, I have spent only the last six years in the Colorado corner of the Four Corners area—only since 2012 have I paid close attention to this weather.

Tragically, too much of the West can now measure climate change by fire. So far in this desert we are spared that marker. But my sons insisted on creating the recommended circle of safety around my cabin by cutting back greasewood, big sagebrush, fourwing saltbush, and two one-seed junipers. We parked a 2,500-gallon water tank on a hill. That water can gravity-flow down to the horse trough, or be used to fill the cisterns if the catchment system isn't working (which it doesn't when there's no rain or snow), or used to fight fire, until everything runs dry.

Including the creek, the flow of which reflects the year's weather, carrying winter's snowfall toward summer if we get snow, tapering down to a trickle, then puddles, if we don't. Monsoons, our other main water source, sometimes start in early July, like last year. But when they start that early, they seem not to carry into September. Like last year. This year they didn't start at all, though two spotty rains caused flashfloods. When the cows come, they will have water—either the creek or, if no more moisture falls, I will haul it in.

The possibility of drought, always hovering in this dry country, is part of why I covet and protect our feed, hauling hay to feed my horses instead of turning them loose to graze the native grasses, hauling hay to supplement the cows. And so I feel annoyed when I get back from town—160 miles round trip—and see in my headlights the red sheen of the Red Angus bull, his big head deep in my haystack.

In the morning, he stands there rooting under the tarp, pulling mouthfuls of hay from the bales, and then pulling the bales themselves out, making an even bigger mess of things. This time I watch as he waddles off to water, a trail starting in his wake as he meanders through the salt-desert shrubs on his way to the creek. He knows where he is going: the gentlest slope toward creek bottom; the low, wide bank from which his bulk can easily stand and drink. This time I don't chase him out, walking the fenceline to look, again, for his entrance.

The place I fixed remains intact. From there I walk up along the outside of the fence, as the bull did, his tracks broad and deep and obvious in the soft soil. He cornered where the fence does, heading west, just ambling, knowing what he was looking for. And, there, he found it, a top wire loose enough that he reared up over it and came down on my side, his tracks left behind to tell the tale.

If I kick him out again, he'll come back in again—he has found the perfect place to winter: free hay, close water. Only problem: me. I text TJ, and she offers to help put the heavy panels up around my precious hay supply. I also get hold of the bull's owner. He'll send his cowboy, Jeff, soon as he can reach him—cell service out here is spotty at best.

TJ comes, and that evening there stands the bull, outside the panels, eating the remains of the hay on the ground. The next morning, soon as it's light enough to see, he appears, munching on hay-scrap leftovers. And there, as I stand in my bathroom getting dressed—which means I'm not dressed—which means I'm naked—rides cowboy Jeff, close enough to the bathroom window to ruin his morning, if he looks.

He doesn't look, thank goodness, and by the time I get outside, the threesome of cowboy, horse, and bull is gone. Their tracks lead over a hill to another gate, and on down the road toward a set of BLM corrals, where Jeff can load the bull into his trailer.

That evening, just the dogs and me and no bull, I feel loneliness descend with the desert darkness—not a porch light on within thirty miles, the only other voice in my world is that of the woodstove pinging its way toward warmth and winter in Disappointment. ⤙

("Getting Ready" is an excerpt from *These Seasons of Disappointment: Cows in the Desert.*)

2018 Finalist

Diana Woodcock

PROJECT DESCRIPTION

The Gobi Desert and its Muslim Inhabitants will articulate the story of the
Gobi Desert and the Hui—how centuries ago Arab Silk Road traders
passed through it en route to the Orient, bringing Islam with them. My
work will capture and juxtapose the calming silence and stark, though
comforting, nature of desert places while also exploring and document-
ing the devastating damage being done as chemical factories disgorge
black plumes of smoke into clear desert air. For nearly eight years, I lived
in Tibet, Macau, and on the Thai-Cambodian border, teaching and working with refugees.

My destination for this research project is the Gobi (Tengger) Desert
in the Chinese Province of Ningxia, Inner Mongolia, where the Gobi
meets the Yellow River.

I will interview Chinese naturalists working to protect endangered
desert species. Since I have lived in China previously (in Tibet, Sichuan
Province/Chengdu, and Macau), I believe that I have developed a needed
degree of patience and sensitivity in communicating with Chinese officials so that I will be granted interviews and permission to visit protected
desert areas.

The project will add a new perspective to the body of desert literature
as it highlights the cross-cultural cooperative spirit (Han and Muslim
Chinese) and the influence of Islam, which regards environmental pres-
ervation and conservation of nature as an integral part of one's faith in
God, in tackling present-day environmental problems.

Arabian Desert Revelations

THE FIRST THING I DID upon arrival was set out a bowl of fresh water, hoping to entice them. For six weeks I waited—no sightings, no sound. Finally one morning I heard squabbling among ubiquitous house sparrows on the roof. Awakened from sleep, I lay in bed smiling. Encouraged, I listened more closely. Ring-necked parakeets at sunset noisily squawked, *I'm passing over!* In date palms, white-cheeked bulbuls sang out their alarms. In acacias, collared and palm doves cooingly boasted of colonizing this Arabian Gulf desert.

I could wonder all day why any bird would stay in these arid conditions—how anything could thrive. I could seek out the sheikhs, look for answers in the Koran or eyes of veiled women in the streets, meditate from dusk till dawn beside a wadi. But I prefer asking black-winged stilts in the reeds by the pond at the date farm, and grey francolins—squat, stub-tailed—along the mangrove verges why we all have these urges to explore new lands, to stay when conditions are so inhospitable and poor.

Choosing to come because I'd lived on the world's rooftop and in lush paradisiacal Thailand but never in the desert, I told myself I'd be fine –I wouldn't waste time missing flora and fauna that couldn't exist in such an arid place as this. By October, the days became more bearable. One morning a dragonfly appeared, dipping her abdomen into the puddle formed by the leaking water tank out back. I would have honored my contract and remained till the end, regardless of feeling at odds with barrenness. But from the moment of the sighting, everything changed—as if furniture in a room had been rearranged to be more inviting. Till then, I had felt persistent hesitation toward settling in, but with the dragonfly's visitation I was home.

❧

"I will seduce my love, lead her into the desert, and speak to
her heart."

—Hosea 2:16

SEDUCED AND LED AS surely as if shackled and noosed, I've wound
up in the desert. But don't get me wrong—this is no wailing song. Far
from it, it's a call for celebration as I acknowledge the soul's penetration
by earth's beauty, creation's oneness. Caught up in the rhythm and flow
of desert seasons, sparseness and apparent emptiness, the heart opens
wide to scarcity, hunger, thirst—and it thrives.

Led into the desert, I quickly learn this is no place for the faint-
hearted. Inborn, biophilic needs awaken. And I, shaken out of
complacency, seek out the secretive ones—follow footprints and body
indentations across the sand. Often I yearn for the Everglades—those
days trolling marsh edges with snowy egrets, marveling how great blue
herons stand frozen for hours stabbing sunfish and gar, how white ibis
grub in the mud for crawfish, how reddish egrets cast wing shadows
over their prey while those ingenious green herons drop fish bits as bait
into the slough—their patience to wait as long as it takes enviable. And
I would trade a thousand nights sleeping on silk sheets, all my treasured books—everything I own but my passion for poetry and life—to
live among those sensual shapely beauties, to be swaddled in the gauzy
purple mists sunrise, sunset as I synthesize with them all the elements of
the grassy river.

But back to the present, the desert, which also is a gift—less flam-
boyant than the Everglades, but once I let the sidra tree speak to me, I
was a goner—the dunes singing, shamal wind ringing the rim of the
Inland Sea. So here, too, I watch and wait for a chance to participate
in synthesis—a guest trying her best not to be invasive in this far from
empty desert on the Arabian Gulf's midwestern coast. I become inspired
by an oil flare-shaped peninsula chiseled by wind and sea, golden-brown
of arid desert, pale cream of coastal salt flats, here and there the green
of farms and date palm plantations. On three sides a sea rousing these
questions: How can it be that exquisitely blue-green? Could windblown

sand alone hone the limestone plateau edges into giant mushrooms and spindly pinnacles? How exactly do green forests of mangroves attract greater flamingos in droves?

As for the dunes—crescent-shaped barchans fifty meters high, long undulating seifs striding southward ahead of the prevailing northwesterly shamal to a tidal lagoon marking the southern border—is it all by Someone's divine order? Taking my time, I wind my way around this coast, determined to make the most of desert living. The shamal blows me away with the dunes—haunts and uplifts, implants a grain to stop my watch on the present moment. I kneel beside the sea as a gull's wings shadow me.

Let me relive again and again several most treasured days at this exquisite zoological crossroads.

❖

An August Day

THE SIDRA TREE SHOOK in the shamal. Nearby a wadi waited for winter rains. Sand-colored gerbils and girds zigzagged between desert squash and acacia. Lesser jerboas hibernated in their subterranean burrows a meter below ground. A Persian nightingale sang its fluty song among a throng of short-toed larks. A rear-fanged sand snake lazed lethargically beside the wadi as the desert gave no hint of Earth's potential for autumn. Dreams of a lusher locale—of apples, pumpkins, plums—whetted my appetite like a mirage. But one succumbs to aridity and scarcity—learns to do without, remembers this is what the Desert Fathers were all about. One day, not a grain of sand stirs—it can be stiflingly still. The next, a shamal wind flings a limb of the sidra against my window pane, shattering glass and shield from the searing sun.

The dried-up wadi waited. A desert wheatear dozed in the acacia's shade. Winter would come again—the rains, wildflowers spreading across the barren waste with lavish fleeting grace—speaking essential truths in the language of delicate blossoms, prying open Earth's unspeakable secrets. And I would understand what the searing sand says. But just then, alone, summer in the desert—birds hiding, keeping silent (save for one bulbul)—I wondered where the caravans were that passed this way, the village by the sea at the desert's verge whose men dived their whole lives for pearls. I hoped for at least one stray camel, one oryx, one palm dove intoxicated on dates, one honey badger to lead me into the shade or a burrow under the sand to sleep through the day-long heat.

Still I would weep—no one more surprised than I—when time came to leave behind the desert. All this desolation. And yet, where the biosphere's thin layer of complexity astounds. Contemplating the desert's stark beauty, my thoughts turned to cities beyond—lakes dying of eutrophication, smelter stacks' acidic emissions killing vegetation, men with oxen (the Industrial Age) digging canals with smoke-belching dredges—reshaping, desecrating whole landscapes. Then thoughts returned to the desert: across the sand, a false cobra left its dimpled pulse of an imprint. Heart of the desert, August's monochrome—nothing to write home about. Brown leaves whirling in a grim garden. Late summer aridity. No clouds. No hope of rain till winter. Flowers had gone to seed. All dust and decay. Vicarious suffering, my body was showing traces. Fulminating sun crackled, shattering the day.

Only at the edge—where expats and wealthy natives live with views of Arabian Gulf waters—do bougainvillea, hibiscus and oleander thrive, fragile blossoms not hardy enough to survive without doting attention of faithful gardeners. But I would be the plain acacia or date palm—self-sufficiently strong. I would embrace the desert, as Rumi advised. I'd cozy up to it as if it were a welcome fire on a wintry afternoon. I'd find my laughter, let it carry me through the flames till I myself became droplets of rain.

⁕

A Day Sleeping Among Bitter Apples

ALL DAY CLOUDS HUNG OVER THE DESERT. Wind blew as if to brew a great storm of hard long rain. But once again, nothing came of them. Beside a wadi I sat and waited, endured hunger and heat, slept among bitter apples—citrulus collocynthis thriving on sandy loam—its perennial root sending forth scabrid vine-like stems. Solitary yellow

flowers bloomed in the leaves' axils. Lemon-sized gourd-like fruit was
filling up with soft white poisonous pulp, in which flat ovate seeds
waited for birds of passage to come and distribute them.

Unable to resist, I tore one from the ground, planning to transplant
it in my garden. But its delicate microscopical leaf structure caused
it to wither within the hour. Clouds still hanging low, wind continuing to blow, I reminisced about its fruit flourishing profusely between
Palestine's mountains and the Mediterranean's eastern shore, from Gaza
to Mt. Carmel—soil and climate all-sufficient for its growth. I took note:
Leave things where they grow.

This was the wild gourd of the Old Testament (II Kings 4:38-40)—
earth gall, exceeding bitterness—and yet, its nutty-flavored seeds taken
from their poisonous enclosure were innocuous. In hard soil, it's widespread. Desert Bedouins grind and make from it a bread. Precious food
source of one Central Saharan tribe – Tibboo Resade – its seeds are
trampled to remove the last traces of bitter pulp, then cleaned by win-
nowing, mixed with ashes from camels' dung, placed on a smooth stone
and rubbed with another to crush the testa. Kernels are sifted, boiled in
water, dried in the sun, then mixed with dried powdered dates. Finally it
becomes palatable and nutritive.

Such is life in the desert: reaching beyond the poisonous enclosure to
what can sustain us.

❧

A Day at an Oasis

TWO HOURS NORTHWEST OF DOHA, his family farm sprawls
hidden behind brick walls. Upon entering, one hears waterfalls—music
to the ears after the silent shifting of sand. Three camels came to nuzzle
me. There were peacocks and ostriches, Arabian horses, ducks and reems,
deer from Australia, cattle, goats, and sheep. No pigs, of course.

My father started with nothing, Hakeem proudly beamed. *Now he owns
six businesses in town.* We sat down to a feast—fresh fish from the Arabian
Gulf, vegetables and lamb from the farm. I heard ducks squabbling on
the pond; I felt the nuzzling of the camels lingering on. Always such a

strange sensation: the awareness of the making of a memory.

Just a few friendly words were exchanged at the Al-Koot Fort. *Come see my farm—you are welcome,* he had smiled—this young man who had studied five years in Tucson, then returned to his Bedouin roots. I could understand if they'd known we were coming, but there we sat unexpectedly. Such impeccable hospitality in the desert: strangers welcomed as if we were emissaries of God—a gift that in the West has all but died. Money surely cannot buy happiness; how many have tried? But at least in the middle of a desert it, can fashion a farm that thrives and a feast fit for Allah.

❧

Returning from Winter Break

I HAVE LIVED ON THE WORLD'S ROOFTOP, TIBET. I have visited the middle of the earth—that archipelago of volcanic islands in the Pacific Ocean, the Galapagos. I think of these places today, hours ticking away toward departure time while I pack to head back to my decade-long home on foreign soil, a desert peninsula surrounded by the Arabian Sea, shifting sands, mangroves of dwindling droves of flamingos. Embraced by desert and sea, I am perfectly placed between them.

Where others see a barren, stark landscape, I continually discover exotica. Where others find the silence unbearable, I hear in my solitude the voices and narratives of the multitude—birds, reptiles, insects. I am touched and changed by sand and salt, shamals and sharkis. I am seduced by dugongs and spiny-tailed agamas, reduced to tears by the sight of a camel carcass half-buried in sand. In mudflats, ghost crabs perform their disappearing acts, and I laugh with joy.

Oh, I did adore the world's rooftop, and I've never stopped hoping to return to the Galapagos. But now this desert ... When winter rains come and flowers appear, I cannot tear myself away. Oh, I know I cannot stay forever. My sojourn here will end. I only meant to stay one year. I well "... understand, life hangs here by a hair."[1] This Arabian Desert's no garden

---

1.   Hafez. "What's Sweeter than a Garden and Good Talk?" (in *Faces of Love*, transl. Dick Davis).

of Eden, Arabian Sea no water of Life—excessively salty. Yet still I see the world in just one of its grains of sand. My heart refuses to grow skittish. After a decade kept from Paradise's shade, I find this desert place still offering amazing grace.

I trace the soul's trinity—from liver to heart to brain.[2] Something of infinity in the desert's pure, unfiltered light. Who needs the constant chaos of clouds? Nowhere is mercy more imminent than in this desert. Oh, the day may come when I wish to run away. But the burning bush— the Leptadenia pyrotechnica—may well hold sway over me. Let it be, if I should stay. But by then, the river country of my birth just might be calling me back. Though some say you can't go home again, the fact is you can do no less than that—the Chesapeake Bay and James in my blood— though for now the mudflats along the Arabian Coast will do just fine.

❖

TO ANYONE CONTEMPLATING a move to the desert, I'd say consider this: a peninsula with Arabian Gulf waters on three sides, an inland sea, flamingos in the shallows, songs of that Persian nightingale—the white-cheeked bulbul—pure magical incantations, the sidra tree spreading its branches like arms raised in praise.

In the silence and solitude, one learns to love one's neighbor for what he is—not for what he claims to be. In this harsh place, one finds within herself the grace of gentleness. Sea lavender will attract one to saline flats otherwise avoided, moorhen and crakes to sewage lagoons hidden by tall green reeds. One may grow so accustomed to arid flat tan terrain till she'll feel like an alien in lush mountains and rain. One settles in, but occasionally the cloud-moving wind will stir the chords of vagabondage, and she'll long for a mountain stream and the wood song. She'll thirst for rain—day-long rain, rain that drenches dreams all night. She'll miss birches and mushrooms.

But there's a seamlessness in all this barrenness—a sand-brown transience that shouldn't be missed: quiet inlets with gentle ripples, springtime with desert hyacinths blossoming, the season of mists when

2. Galen said there are three kinds of soul – located in the liver, heart and brain.

the desert scrub drips with moisture. This is the place to enter the cloister of one's own design — take all the time one needs to simply be.

One moment spent observing the desert monitor lizard sunning itself on a kopje, and the emptiness of worldly existence overwhelms. Silence, stillness astounds. The time comes to trade one's downy bed for a hard lodging. Tired of living half-dead, one keeps eyes wide open—finds her own flat-topped solitary spot in the sun.

At least that's how it's been for me. I often hear myself laughing like the gulls I keep company with on the desert's moist lip. Feet touching sand, I whirl in my patched frock—arms outstretched like wings of red-crowned cranes. When I hear someone whisper, She's *gone insane,* I smile. Chiffon dresses given away, I've let the winds replace my tambourines. No need now of *wasta*[3] or the mathematics of probability, I'm content beside a wadi in the shade of a sidra tree. ☙

3.   Arabic for influence or having connections

(Note: "Arabian Desert Revelations" is a new work submitted for this anthology.)

2017 Winner

Naseem Rakha

PROJECT DESCRIPTION

In India, the tortoise, Akaupara, is believed to carry the Earth on its back. In North America, the Iroquois believe the tortoise is the source of creation. The Chinese have similar myths, as did the ancient Greeks. I am submitting my application for this award to research and write about the West's desert tortoises and what I might learn from these long-lived, slow-moving, and widely venerated creatures.

The desert tortoise has ranged in the Sonoran and Mojave deserts for more than 20 million years. In the 1950's, their population was estimated at 200 hundred adults per square mile. Since then, human encroachment and predation have decreased their presence by as much as 90 percent. Today the desert tortoise is listed as threatened with risk of extinction.

My project goal is to explore what the desert tortoise and its habitat teach about intention and quiet; what creation myths about the creature teach about the value of story and its place in our psyche; and most importantly, what we must do to support the desert tortoise and its habitat so that it too does not vanish into pure myth.

My plan is to spend the autumn and winter of 2017 working with biologists from Joshua Tree National Park and the US Fish and Wildlife Service to better understand the life-cycle and habitat needs of desert tortoises, and then take what I learn on a solo journey into the desert during the spring of 2018 to search for the imperiled tortoise.

The product of this work will be included in a book of essays I hope to have published about the American West and what its deserts teach about history, culture, time, space, patience and beauty. The book is already in progress, and my intent is to give readers reasons to devote their attention and passion to the quiet presence of the desert and its rarefied inhabitants.

Everything Is Temporary

IT'S A WEEKDAY, I THINK. It's a weekday in December in the year 2015, and I am deep in the Grand Canyon, just thirty feet above the Colorado River. Not far above me is a twisted outcrop of columnar basalt. The hardened lava protrudes right and left, up and down. Some of its columns are as gnarled as tree roots, some shoot outward—spines on a sea urchin, rays of the sun, ion trails cast by dying stars.

I've been in the Canyon for nineteen days now. I began my journey at Lee's Ferry, floated under Navajo Bridges, through Marble Canyon, past Redwall Cavern, the Bridge of Sighs, Nankoweap, the Little Colorado, Horn Creek Rapid, Hermit Rapid, Crystal, Kanab. I have eleven more days left on this trip through the base of this desert world, eleven more nights to sleep under a sky wrapped by the Milky Way's diaphanous scarf, eleven more opportunities to absorb all I can from this primitive, bare-knuckled world and the quiet it holds.

The desert is my muse, the place I come to learn what lies beneath my skin. Pavement people, deciduous dwellers, cultivators of copious gardens, they do not understand my fascination with the desert. High or low. Cold or hot, its telltale surface is poetry to me. Its ambient light a kind of god. *It's pretty,* these people say. *It's vast and certainly unusual and the sky, yes, it is big, but don't you miss the green?* There's green, I say. *But what about rain? Don't you miss the rain?* There's rain, I say. *Yes, but it's so, well—barren. There's nothing there. Just rock and dust, so much dust and sand and scorpions and don't even get started on the snakes...* That's when I smile. It's not for everyone, I say.

There are just fifteen of us on this river trip. All of us strangers to one another before we came together three weeks ago in Flagstaff on the night of a blizzard. The permit holder had cobbled together the group, struggling to find people willing or able to go. Now we fifteen are rivermates, working as one to move ourselves, a couple tons of food and gear, and four rafts, two dories, two kayaks down 289 miles of winter river. Short days, long freezing nights, ice-covered dawns—we are a tribe isolated by mile-high walls that keep the chaos and distractions of the rim-world at bay. There are no cell signals deep in the Canyon, no interpretive waysides, no Netflix or radios. The last time we saw anyone from outside our tribe was ten days ago, on the shore of Unkar's sandy delta, where the Ancient Ones once carved out terraces on which to grow corn and beans. On the day we saw the other group of rafters, a haboob—a desert windstorm—had hit, and the rafters were huddled in the mesquite and tamarisk risking the prick of thorns in order to shelter themselves from the assault of the wind-born sand. Our group was on the river, one person on each oar, fighting our way down through the Unkar rapid as the wind tried to force us back up. Since that day, we haven't seen anyone but ourselves, so it's easy to imagine we're the only ones left on the planet, but for the slash of contrails against the lazurite sky, and, of course, the daily river surges—tides determined not by nature but by the power demands of far-flung cities.

Still, I've found no better place than the Grand Canyon to separate myself from the friction of the world. The daily rub of sights and sounds that constantly erode. The news and neighbors and needs, always the needs, and the traffic and the crime and the bills and the ills, so many ills, and the Girl Scouts with their cookies, and the Mormons with their missions, and the politicians with their smiles, and all the aisles of things and things and things that end up in landfills or as plastic islands the size of small countries, floating in a forgotten sea. All of it rubbing until a numbness sets in. And an apathy. And a kind of modern-age depression born from a sense of powerlessness. A weakness so overwhelming that when a personal crisis hits, it is hard to get up off the ground.

The invitation to join this winter trip came at the right time. My father had died. He died, and there was this hole, you see. A place where my father had been, and now he was gone and I had no idea how to deal with this loss, this hole, this sense of being plunged into a new and far lonelier world. I needed perspective. I needed silence. I needed time. I needed to be in the presence of something larger than my grief. So I accepted a trip to a place that promised to be cold, and dark, and raw— and very, very deep.

❧

I PAUSE IN MY HIKE TO SIT on a ledge above the Colorado.
Beneath me, boulders are hammered by cascades of white water. The
sound is open mouthed and large. I open my backpack, dig out a
sandwich and water bottle. As I drink, I watch a raven circle then land
on a nearby ledge. His eyes are on my sandwich. I smile. (Ravens are
audacious robbers. I've had one break into my backpack, steal a piece
of dried papaya, then fly over to me and gloat about it, the pilfered treat
hanging from its beak like an orange cigar.) *I'm not sharing,* I shout over
the roar of the river. I bite into my sandwich menacingly, and the bird
puffs out his feathers and flies up and up the Canyon walls until he is too
tiny to see.

Once, when I was about four years old, my father woke me at dawn.
Come with me, he said. Our family lived in Chicago in an apartment with
a view of the Loop the to the north and Lake Michigan to the east, and
as I followed my father into the living room I saw for the first time how
the rising sun poured its color into the lake—rose and peach and orange
and maroon. I pointed and my father nodded, then he led me out onto
our small balcony, and even now I can feel the sensations of standing out
there—the smell of the air, the coolness of the spring breeze against my
thin pajamas. It felt like we, my father and I, were on the wing of a plane
gliding through the pale morning light. But what I remember most about
that morning, what has stuck and what I look forward to still, were the
sound of birds—hundreds, perhaps thousands of them singing to the
rising sun, as my father and I stood there hand in hand, listening.

I pull out my binoculars, scan the layer-cake surface of the surrounding rock walls. It wasn't a huge leap for me, a child who habitually
collected and labeled rocks, to one day become a geologist. My degree
solidified my fascination with the formations on the earth. Everything
from the tiny creatures that make up the oolitic limestone that lined the
shores near my alma mater in Illinois, to these walls now. In my view,
nothing lessens the burden of historical or even personal loss more than
having it weighed on the scale of geologic time. At Lee's Ferry, where I've
begun all my Grand Canyon river trips, the surrounding rock is approximately two hundred million years old. Within a mile, the boater has

floated fifty million years deeper into the past into the fossil-rich Kaibab
Limestone, created when the region was an inland sea. Eight-tenths of a
mile further, and the Kaibab is out of reach as the river carves deeper and
deeper into the Earth, through limestones and sandstones and shales
and conglomerates: one thousand eight hundred million years, stacked
like bricks.

⌁

How long would it take to count to a million?
Eleven days—no eating nor sleeping.
How long would it take to count to a billion?
Thirty years.
How long would it take to count out the years of my father's life?
Less than ninety seconds.

⌁

I FINISH MY SANDWICH and pack away my water bottle, zip up
my backpack. The basalt I am sitting amid is a relative newcomer in
this place. It is part of the Uinkaret Lava Field, a series of more than
two hundred volcanoes that reshaped this area between 3.6 million to
one thousand years ago. These particular rocks are likely from Vulcan's
Throne, a thousand-foot cinder cone which sits on the north rim of the
Canyon, just east of where I am now. Vulcan's Throne is thought to have
formed a mere 73,000 years ago—barely a baby's first breath, geologically speaking.

Still, I have to wonder what this place was like back then. How
wide was the river? What grew here, what prowled, what grazed? What
was the first sign that the dome growing on the edge of the north rim
was about to release millions of metric tons of blood-red lava into
this writhing river? Usually, pillars of columnar basalt either stand
in formation like soldiers, or lie horizontally, as orderly as cordwood.
Instead, these distorted stones shout pandemonium, clashing forces,
disarray. This is lava that danced with water, curled into eddies, pooled
in shoals, dammed the river, and was ultimately broken by the water's

inexorable flow. The result is what I am standing next to now, the churning, chocolatey froth of Lava Falls. Its twenty-foot waves heave over sharp-toothed boulders, smashing into them with concussive force, while its icy claws slash at anyone fool enough to try to make their way through.

Long before any Grand Canyon river trip commences, boaters anticipate the moment they will meet Lava Falls, the most dangerous rapid in the canyon. They study rafting books, watch videos, compare notes. Which is better, entering at high water or low? Taking the left run or the right? What about the lateral waves that wait at the bottom? How do you avoid the raft-eating holes?

Just yesterday, we were rowing toward Lava Falls. A mile up river, the water was calm. Silently, we drifted. A half-mile further, the water was still calm. A canyon wren sang. A heron flew by.

But then something subtle occurred. First, there was a shift in air pressure, a tightening around our ear drums. Next, came a subterranean hum which gained strength with each passing moment. By the time we stopped to scout the rapid, the sound of still unseen rapid had grown into a hungry growl. We hiked along the river's edge, climbed up a cliff, and then looked down.

Beneath us was a maelstrom. A chaos. A cross between hell, and whatever lives right next to hell. From above, we could distinguish various routes, but all of them were iffy, and none would be visible once we were back at river level looking out toward the water's horizon where the river suddenly fell out-of-sight. A misjudged angle, an overcompensated drag on an oar, anything at all, and a raft, or dory, or kayak would be swallowed by the waiting holes.

We trudged back to our boats, made sure everything was secure, tightened our life vests, and one by one left the shore, then pushed our boats forward. Within moments the red silt water sucked us down and tossed us into the air, grabbed at our oars, bludgeoned our boats, knocked us sideways and silly until suddenly it was done, and the unsatisfied river spat us out still upright.

Another group of fortunate fools.

WE HONORED OUR SUCCESSFUL RUN through Lava Falls with
a layover, unpacking the boats in the early afternoon with plans to stay
on the beach not one, but two nights. So today, I have hiked back to the
falls in hopes of seeing a different group take its turn with Lava Falls. In
the summer months, this would not be a long wait. Commercial trips
embark from Lee's Ferry four or five times a day, many of them carrying
three times the number of people as we have on our trip now. Those summer trips are floating parties with young, well-tanned and hardy boat
people serving a well-heeled group of tourists as they scream through
this Canyon. These groups never have the opportunity to do what I have
done so many times already on this winter journey: just sit, just watch,
just think, just feel. Just hike up a side canyon to see where it might go.
Just watch a rapid, or a raven, or the light move over a stone.

My father visited the Grand Canyon twice in his life. The first time
was in 1957, when he and some other students from Purdue University,
all of them Indian immigrants, borrowed a car and drove from Indiana
out west. The second time was in 2006 when my brother had driven him
across the country to come live near me and my husband and our child
in Oregon. My mother had died, and my father had been keeping vigil
over her memory in their house in Illinois. He would not sleep in the
bed they'd shared, could not listen to their classical music without crying. Every week, he would go to the cemetery and lay yellow roses on her
grave. My father, whose faith was in curiosity and science and math, the
mystery of the stars, the beauty of the human spirit, the songs of birds,
went to the Canyon, looked over its edge and said it confirmed his belief
that all things are temporary. A whisper in the wind. A negligible speck of
sand.

᠁

I STARE UPRIVER, WILLING A FLOTILLA of yellow rafts to
appear. But none do, so I turn my attention to the contorted outcrop I'd
seen earlier. It is a couple hundred feet above where I sit, so I strap on my
pack and start to scramble up a scree slope to get a closer look. But scree
is unfriendly terrain, and my footing is poor. I grab a nettle plant to stop
a fall, feel its sting; I scrape against a fishhook barrel cactus, feel a spine

embed in my thigh. I slip and slide and call myself stupid, but I climb on. Finally, I reach the outcrop and haul myself over the top.

Beside me on this ledge is a dead and desiccated barrel cactus. The living one—the one whose spine is still lodged in my leg—was strikingly beautiful, with four-inch-long yellow and magenta spines. But this one, this dead and desiccated one, also has a certain beauty. Its body is ashen and has collapsed in on itself; its spines, no longer alive with color, stick out like rusted nails. In this brittle environment, where decay is slow, the cactus may have died a decade ago, maybe even more. I know from its size it lived at least ninety years, nine decades surrounded by a landscape that dwarfs any imagination of time and space.

❧

THREE DAYS BEFORE WE reached Lava Falls, we had stopped at River Mile 136.9, where I climbed several hundred feet above Deer Creek Falls to a soft and sinuous chamber cut into the 500 million-year-old Tapeats Sandstone that makes up that side canyon. The chamber walls are tall and warped and layered like coils of hand-worked pottery. The creek, Deer Creek, is small and clear and melodic. It gathers in pools, then drops. Gathers in pools, then drops again. Every Grand Canyon river trip I've been on, I've taken time here. It feels sacred to me, this cloister. An umbilical link from the Earth's very heart to the outside world. I climbed up, and I sat by myself, and thought of how my father would have loved this place and how he would have pressed me, his geologist daughter, to tell him about its origins. And how we would have talked about time and space and the infinite magnitude of the universe and all it held. And while I sat there, a water ouzel—a dull-gray robin-sized bird, John Muir's favorite—played in a pool, and did what it is most known for—sing and sing and sing. That's when I reached into my pocket and pulled out the pill bottle. I had been carrying it every day of the trip, waiting for the right time. And that was it. That moment, right then, with the careening sun slipping through the narrow gap between the canyon walls, lighting the water, the leaves of a lone cottonwood, the ouzel and its spray, that was the moment I opened the bottle, reached over the water, and sprinkled out its contents. Some of my father's ashes sank to the sand, some lapped onto the shore, and some, the lightest, most crystalline specks, swirled around like the numbers in a Fibonacci sequence, the whorl of a nautilus, a spiral galaxy—and then floated away.

I came to the Grand Canyon because I needed time, I needed quiet, and I needed the perspective that comes from desert walls. I needed the dry space where the roots of the earth remind me all things are temporary. Heartaches, heart attacks, politics, preachy puritans, guns, laws, dams, disease.

Canyons.

Rivers.

Stone.

Everything is stardust, my father once said as we looked at a night sky. Borrowed pieces of light, elemental and beautiful and bright. ⬟

2017 Finalist

Kendra Atleework

PROJECT DESCRIPTION

(Note: This book, *Sweetwater: Life and Change in the Rain Shadow of the Sierra Nevada,* will be published in 2020 by Algonquin Books.)

In February of 2015, a wildfire raged through the brush that covers the floor of Owens Valley, destroying much of my childhood neighborhood. The fire spared my childhood house but reduced many of my neighbors' homes to ash. Part memoir, part travel narrative, and part researched investigation, my manuscript follows the rebuilding process while journeying through the public, personal, and natural history of Owens Valley.

My subject is a place of extremes: a high desert valley surrounded to the east and west by mountains rising over 14,000 feet. Rainfall averages five inches a year and can be as low as zero. In 1913, a 233-foot aqueduct began carrying the valley's lone river south to Los Angeles, turning the valley from irrigated farmland back into desert and forever changing the local economy and culture. Like many in Owens Valley, my father, a mapmaker and retired hot air balloon pilot, embraces a creative lifestyle in order to inhabit such a harsh and remote region. The resulting community is complicated and unique.

The writing sample is an excerpt from a chapter of *Sweetwater* that explores the tension of living in an arid region, investigating the increasing variability of climate and my own relationship to an ever-shifting environment. I narrate part of this chapter from my teenage perspective, when the loss of the valley's water felt like a plain and simple theft. Later in the book, this story of villain and victim complicates as I begin to recognize a chain of predation.

My book will depict water in Owens Valley as a living issue and a microcosm for how we relate to the desert, conveying an ongoing struggle to readers and emphasizing that the water transfer still presents complex challenges to environmentalists and to the Owens Valley Paiutes' way of life.

Sweetwater

IT WAS EVENING, POP TELLS ME, when the well went dry. Mid-November deep in drought, the days growing shorter without losing the heat of early fall. In the kitchen, he put a glass under the faucet and flicked the handle. First, nothing. Then a choking noise from the pipes beneath the sink, while outside in the backyard, forty feet below the roots of the dry lawn, the electric pump at the bottom of the well began to drag at the air. Without water to cool its moving parts, a pump burns up in sixty seconds. My father grabbed at the breaker box on the wall in the hallway. He saved the pump, but after that the house was without water, at least in the way we are used to having water. A little trickled back around the pump from the aquifer if Pop and my stepmother waited, and water ran from a faucet for two minutes at a time before the pump threatened to burn up again. In the granite-walled shower the pipes hacked after a minute and left you with soap in your eyes. The water in Owens Valley is soft and tastes like the frozen top of a mountain, but there just isn't enough.

In 1903, Mary Austin called the deserts of California "a big mysterious land, a lonely, inhospitable land, beautiful, terrible," and three years into a hard drought her words feel especially true. Owens Valley is a place defined by lack of moisture. Dry wind buffeted the windows of the house where I grew up, crisping the wave out of my mother's hair, and as a child I didn't know what it was to sweat. Our bodies existed in states of nosebleeds and cracked skin on knuckles. I grew up beside blue-bellied lizards bobbing on rocks, a velvet ant that stung my sister's finger when she reached down to stroke its white fur, fat black widows that lived in the wooden frame of our old hot tub. Pop's neck, where shade from his hat does not reach, is leathery as the skin of the lizards I chased. The amount of rain Owens Valley gets in a good year would equate to apocalyptic drought east of the 100th meridian.

Easterners and Midwesterners cannot fathom the desert in a bad year.

In Owens Valley, snowmelt runs from streams called tributaries into a single river flowing north to south. This river used to empty into a lake one hundred feet long and deep enough to ferry steam boats to silver mines. Now, Los Angeles reroutes the river into an aqueduct. Owens Lake has been dry for almost a century, its water carried 233 miles south to the city in a steel pipeline nine feet high and wide. The wind billows pale alkaline and arsenic powder across the lakebed and into the lungs of those in surrounding towns, making Owens Valley the dustiest place in North America.

Usually, snow melting out of the mountains seeps into the ground, replenishing the aquifer, but for months, to keep the city running through drought, Los Angeles rerouted tributary creeks directly into the aqueduct—creeks normally allowed to wind through my Owens Valley hometown of Bishop and saturate the ground before joining the river. The earth became a squeezed sponge, and the aquifer dropped below the reach of old wells like my father's.

This used to be an agricultural valley, but after the city began piping the water away in 1913, the fields died. Ranchers still raise cattle and grow alfalfa, but most of them do so on land leased from LA, their water carefully metered. The cottonwoods planted as windbreaks before the water table sank below their roots lie silvery on the valley floor. Many of those who could afford to leave the valley, left. Some of the wealthiest people in LA got richer off of development, as land in Southern California became arable, and desert was displaced to the north.

My father has lived most of his life in a place where water constitutes the most notable export, and in Owens Valley folks are viscerally aware of its journey south. Our river runs scarce and spoken for. Put your hands in the current and know that the water will travel far—through desert, then into a chemical bath, city pipes, and finally through storm drains and out to the sea. It passes between your fingers for a moment, but this water is swiftly moving on.

A MONTH AFTER THE WELL went dry, while a drill rig rumbled in the yard and my father and stepmother filled buckets with the neighbor's hose, I made a visit home from Minneapolis. It was the heart of the coldest winter in Minnesota in thirty-five years and the warmest in California since we started keeping track in 1895. Even without drought, coming home means remembering dryness. "The evaporation from the body was so rapid that a man might drop in his tracks with water in his canteen," Mary Austin wrote of a desert not far from Owens Valley. How startling to remove bread from its wrapping and feel it turn stale before you can spread jam. On a diagram of precipitation, Owens Valley is colored dark red, the shade used by the Western Regional Climate Center to indicate one-to-five inches of annual rainfall. Bishop, too small to register on most maps, is recognized as the third driest city in the country, behind Las Vegas and Yuma, Arizona, drier than any part of Utah, New Mexico, or the Great Plains.

In western states, drought is a part of the fabric of climate. From 1976 to 1977, virtually no rain fell in California. Chinook salmon and striped bass bobbed and rotted in the warm, shallow rivers, and seven million trees died in Sierra Nevada forests. In some places, three of every four conifer succumbed to bark beetles, root rot, or fire. Farmers tore out rice paddies and grain fields and planted drought-resistant crops like barley and wheat. Lakes and reservoirs fell too low for fishing, the sides of the mountains were too dry for skiing, and Californians drilled nine thousand new water wells.

In Bishop, the year I was born was the driest on record, until 2013. In August of 1989 my parents took me home, past Pioneer Cemetery, past Mt. Tom and its skirt of brown meadows, along the stretch of highway that led to our cabin, and put me in a crib in their bedroom with a view of volcanic bluffs and Jeffrey pines. That year, 1.8 inches of rain fell in Owens Valley. Groundwater dropped, mule deer moved higher into the mountains. Jackrabbits and coyotes panted over dry washes. All the time, the river flowed into the aqueduct, and the aqueduct flowed south.

IN THE PRECIOUS DAYS I HAVE to spend in California, I sit on a stool in the kitchen, my elbows on the counter, and I listen to my father. As the drill rig chugs out the sliding glass door, Pop tells me the well will be done any day now, maybe even today. He doesn't sound relieved— more like he can't believe it. He stands at the stove, browning corn tortillas in a pan.

I reach across the counter for a map, one made by my father. It is his business to keep local gas stations and visitor centers supplied with maps and guidebooks, keep the tourists on safe roads. This copy of the *Bishop Region Recreation Topo Map & Guide* is marked with black ink where Pop drew a curving path, guiding a friend to the start of a hiking trail. I can picture the dirt road he marked, dusty, leading through the desert to the base of a fifteen-hundred-foot rock pile, good for scrambling and trail running. Pop doesn't need to use his own maps much anymore. They're imprinted in his head, but I like to spread them out and look at them, see the roads and mountains distilled to ink. I like the weight of the paper and the colors, sage green and tan, matching the terrain. City maps are a mesh of right angles and street names, but my father's maps show mountains and a flat valley floor.

Unfold one. Smooth the paper, waterproof and tear resistant, good for campers and hikers who submit themselves to the whims of desert and mountain weather—I have climbed a peak in July to find myself pelted by gum balls of hail and fled the summit amidst lightning. A map must be strong. The shaded relief of mountains hems the valley east and west, elevations noted at twelve thousand, fourteen thousand feet.

Highway 395 meanders. At the northeastern corner of the map, black dashes form the state line, dividing Esmeralda and Mono counties, where the Boundary Peak Wilderness of Nevada gives way to the White Mountain Wilderness of California. The names of the streams and peaks call to be arranged into stanzas, full of rhyme and alliteration: Sand Canyon, Cardinal Pinnacle, Cottonwood Creek. This is the language I was first taught to love. Blind Springs Hill, Sherwin Crest, Round Valley, Onion Valley, Bear Creek Spire, Mt. Starr. Owens River runs a thin blue groove, cutting through the gorge, thickening briefly at Pleasant Valley Reservoir and curving past the tiny Bishop airport, around town.

In this moment I remember summer, nine years ago. My best friend Elizabeth and I are out of school. We work the dinner shift at a greasy-spoon cafe, where every day we scurry between tables for eight hours, clock out, bundle our tips into Altoid tins, and pass between dark mountains to swim in this river.

Elizabeth drives. In Bishop, the lights of Main blaze but the stores are closed, all except Kmart and Vons grocery, set side-by-side behind an oversized parking lot, over which the sky appears very black. The lot stretches so enormous as to lie almost empty—the developers were not local—so that everyone drives across spaces and lanes, cutting diagonally over the blacktop, ignoring reversed arrows and solid yellow lines. To do otherwise would be to trace an absurd maze around imaginary obstacles. Open space demands originality. It took me years in the city to remember that traffic laws do, in fact, apply in parking lots.

Elizabeth has long black hair. She is tall like me, and her fingers are thin. When she was little she used to try to run away from home. She cut the heads off dead ravens and speared them on sticks and drilled the sticks into the dirt at the side of the highway. She swallows the anger of this valley, and it makes her glow.

She turns east on Line Street and we pass the Mexican restaurant where the waitress calls her *mijita,* and she knows she can get margaritas without being carded—where I drink tamarind Jalisco sodas at her side because I am not adventurous in the same ways. Then we're into the desert, where cottonwoods stand in ghostly clusters along the river, unmissable sentries in this valley of brush.

Two mustangs, Whisper and Max, drowse in corrals not far from the river. Elizabeth convinced her father to buy the mustangs, allegedly caught in the deserts of the Great Basin. I ride with her and we come home with straw in our pockets, smelling of horses. Neither of us has a clue what we're doing. We trot short distances from the corral without saddles as the horses' hooves sink in sand.

On a dirt road that parallels Owens River the car chatters over washboard, windows down so we can smell the water, music loud—acoustic guitars, pining voices, Cat Stevens, Tracy Chapman.

We pass the tall ghost of an abandoned grain silo into which I peered once, down to the bottom through a hole in the wall, and saw a pile of dead raccoons.

Elizabeth puts a hand into the warm night, and her black hair flies with the dust.

Though the river on the outskirts of Bishop doesn't carry the quantities of water it did one hundred years ago, most years it still swells with spring snowmelt, and tall grasses grow around its banks. Here, the air has the clean smell of mud and the rotten smell of reeds mulching in the shallows. Cattle wade, and cottonwoods sink their roots. Years before, my parents loaded inner tubes into our Land Cruiser, and the five of us jumped off a bridge into water that was deep and cold. We floated four miles south to Warm Springs Road, as the rubber smudged our skin. We passed deflated tubes lolling in low branches, and Pop called us back when we drifted too close to the snarl at the river's edge. *Stay out of the willows! Don't get popped!*

We broke cattails apart, and the fluffy seed vessels stuck to our skin like fur. Floating on our backs, limbs draped over the tubes, we glimpsed miles of brush beyond the banks. All the time we could see mountains, east and west, standing guard.

AT MY FATHER'S KITCHEN COUNTER, I trace our old inner tube course on paper. On Pop's map the river seems ancient, immovable. It has washed through this valley for three quarters of a million years. But there's another line here: gray, almost graceful, dipping in and out of sight.

The pipeline.

When I was hardly taller than the sill I used to look out the windows of our house at the northern lip of Owens Valley, partway up the mountains, and watch heat waves rise and follow the pipeline until it disappeared south between the White Mountains and the Sierra Nevada.

I can't remember a time when I didn't understand the movement of water in this valley: always south, always away. *The aqueduct is like a gun*, Pop first explained. The pipeline begins at Grant Lake, sixty miles north of Bishop, where it collects water from tributary creeks like Lee Vining, Parker, Walker and Rush. Here, it enters a tube—*like a gun barrel*. The pipeline burrows underground and runs to the Crowley Dam, then tunnels to Owens River Gorge, where the water falls over three turbine generators, spitting over the tuff walls of the canyon—then through a cement-lined canal, open to the sky, snaking past Bishop. For awhile Owens River parallels the canal, and water remains in the river for fishing, floating, dropping off a rope swing. The canal meets Owens River forty miles south of Bishop, and here it picks up all the valley's water, leaving the riverbed nearly dry.

The canal becomes a steel aqueduct and moves south with the

conviction of gravity. In the end, water from Owens Valley travels 233 miles, a five-hour drive through the desert, to LA.

Outside in the yard, the drill rig hums, dulled by the glass door. In the kitchen, Pop cuts carrots, and sunshine filters over him through the skylight. Across the counter I examine a postcard I bought at Manor Market, along with eggs from Bishop coops and tomatoes from the Central Valley. The aisles of Manor Market are narrow, the shelves packed with jars of salsa, soy milk and cheese. Teenagers push mops over the floor. Outside, battered trucks fill up at the pumps. A giant plastic rooster perches on the roof.

I found the postcard in a counter rack. The picture shows two men beside a creek in a cow- spotted pasture, swinging shovels at each other's heads. The caption reads, "Discussing water rights, a western pastime." I slide the postcard across the counter to Pop, and he turns from the stove and smiles. He says, *whiskey's for drinking. Water's for fighting over.*

Years ago, floating on our backs in that river, Elizabeth and I could not remember, nor had we even seen pictures, of the valley covered by forty thousand acres of crops and orchards. Yet Bitterness lingered, like humidity in damper places. In a copy of the local paper, the *Inyo Register,* I've read a letter to the editor that references LA's presence in Owens Valley as "colonial rule" and "exploitation as usual." The word "stole" floats around during water talks at community meetings. The local air pollution control district negotiates constantly with the city regarding the amount of dust allowed to billow from the lakebed, and people my father's age are a long way from forgetting the 1980s, when Mono Lake, seventy miles north of Bishop, would have gone the way of Owens Lake if locals hadn't waged legal war.

After dark in September of 1976, two boys from Owens Valley used a crowbar to break into a shed on the valley floor containing equipment for the maintenance of wilderness trails. From it they took two cases of dynamite, blasting caps and twenty feet of fuse.

Surely the boys knew the tradition of Owens Valley ranchers, who attacked the pipeline seventeen times between 1924 and 1931, laying dynamite by moonlight. In November of 1924, seven hundred valley folks camped for four days by a set of steel doors called the Alabama Gates, beside the dry lakebed. The gates control the flow of water in the canal that leads into the aqueduct. The occupiers opened the gates, and water coursed back into the lake. Legend has it when a carload of armed detectives arrived from the city, the local sheriff headed them off at the highway and told them, "You go over there and start trouble, don't expect to come back alive." The city sent a court injunction instead, a stack of papers the sheriff delivered, and the ranchers threw the pages in the water. They pitched tents, grilled a bed of cooking coals, and threw a party.

Fifty-two years later, the boys found the Alabama Gates in darkness and ran before they heard the explosion.

They were young, one still in high school, and I believe they resembled Elizabeth and me—angry at something they couldn't catch or see or understand. Thousands of people from somewhere else flowed through our towns year round and made our economy viable, leaving money on the gummy tables of the burger joint where we worked and cheeseburger cartons on the side of the highway. When I was little, a drunk driver from out of town killed a local family on the road we drove daily to and from school. In the days that followed, the town mourned as one organism.

Just after midnight that September in 1976, the sheriff found a crowd gathered beside the Alabama Gates, cheering. Often, in Owens Valley, the moon shines so brightly it throws shadows.

Perhaps a moon rose over the Inyo Mountains, and the sheriff saw water, ten million gallons flowing from the aqueduct, wetting the long-dry lakebed.

"We'd all thought about doing something like that, but they actually hauled off and did it," a woman who worked in a local gas station told the *LA Times*. "So we gave them rousing shoulder punches and clinked beer bottles in their honor." The father of one of the boys is alleged to have told a neighbor, before he learned the culprit was his son, "If I ever find out who bombed the gates, I'll buy him a steak dinner."

How must the water have looked, on any of those nights, forty years ago or ninety, dampening the desert floor, flooding the dens of burrowing owls? It's something Elizabeth and I imagined all those nights as the current tangled our hair, the river not yet a penned and caught thing.

A river may take many forms, lending some element of that form to the people whose country it traverses. In 1930, the urban design firm

Olmstead and Bartholomew recommended that LA connect its beaches and mountains with a 440-mile network of undeveloped land, and that some of this land run the course of the LA River, forming a flood plain during wet seasons and a public park when the climate was dry. Open land along the super-urban path of the river could be easily accessed by the families who lived nearby, families who did not have time or money or cars to travel to beaches and mountain reserves, and so lived only in built worlds. Undeveloped land along the river could also give a home to disappearing plants native to California.

At the turn of the nineteenth century, Mary Austin visited LA and was "daunted by the wrack of the lately 'busted' boom...the unwatered palms had a hurt but courageous look, as of young wives when they first suspect that their marriages may be turning out badly." She was frightened by the "evidences of planlessness, the unimaginative economic greed, the idiot excitation of mere bigness." Austin witnessed the early blinking of a city that grew to send its population clambering north, fresh from the backyard pool but hungry for a black sky over mountains or a big moon, bright stars, for the huge and empty, a parking lot you can sail through without a care.

It was not interesting to the city to facilitate the meeting of the poor families and the native plants of California; it was not appealing to make public 100,000 acres of private land, and the plan to leave the LA River undeveloped died under pressure from the Southern Pacific Railroad, the Los Angeles Times, and various powerful Angelenos, many of the same entities who grew rich when Owens Valley water came to the city. The LA River was "armored," paved in a narrow channel that carried storm runoff to the sea and allowed industrial development right up to its concrete banks.

Fourteen years after the completion of the aqueduct, LA's population grew to one million. Between 1920 and 1930, Bishop's population fell from 1,304 to 850. The number of local farms dropped by sixty percent. The yearly value of agricultural production dropped from more than four million dollars to less than one million. If these numbers feel abstract, consider the percentage of folks who must have known one another in a town of thirteen hundred, must have borrowed eggs and tended irrigation ditches together. Gather more than half of your neighbors in the auditorium of your imagination. Now imagine them gone. No one buys their houses; their houses fall apart slowly while you watch. Owens Valley became a backyard for LA tourists, an outpost for the agencies that manage this "metropolitan hinterland," and the old life of the valley existed only in memory, and then only in imagining.

Owens River turns and doubles back, and when you float on your back on an inner tube on a summer afternoon you may believe it has no end, but it does. It ends in the aqueduct, and from there it goes away.

With the car doors open so we can still hear music, Elizabeth and I float in darkness. Our campfire spreads gold scraps over the water. The cold unclenches the knots in our feet, the wind stirs the cottonwoods, and between the leaves we see stars. Here, we drift until after midnight.

And here, we make a point to pee in the river.

"Take that, LA," Elizabeth says. "How do you like our water now?" ⌖

2017 Finalist

Charles Hood

PROJECT DESCRIPTION

"Red Center" is focused on the Lambert Centre, one of the most remote locations in Australia. The middle of nowhere is always the center of somewhere, and I want to write a love letter to nothingness, based on a ten-mile radius of the Lambert marker.

There will be a lot to cover. With no wildlife surveys published yet, my site overview will need to include lichen, birds, meteorites, night skies, ephemeral pools, now-abandoned ranching stations, Aboriginal history, feral animals like camels and native ones like long-eared bats, and ornery plants like spinifex—a four-way mix of yucca, sandpaper, broken glass, and sheer cussed tenacity. For models I much admire books like Bill Fox's *Playa Works* and Kim Stringfellow's *Jackrabbit Homestead,* but I want to go even deeper into natural history and geology—another working title in my mind is "core sample," if that metaphor can be expanded to imply not just drilling down but looking straight up and following vision all the way to outer space.

Note: The following writing by Charles Hood is an updated work in lieu of his original submission. An earlier version of this essay appeared in *The Devil's Punchbowl: A Cultural & Geographic Map of California Today,* Red Hen Press, 2010.)

Mono Lake

FROM OUTER SPACE IT LOOKS like a road-killed blue donut,
roughly ten miles by ten, with a black volcano in the middle covered by
the dirty confetti of 80,000 connubial seagulls. Mono Lake exists on
the high, Tibetan steppe of a sagebrush desert and, from Highway 395, it
looks like a pond on the moon, all the more so as you swing down closer
and start to pass the first stucco spires of tufa, a cross between movie
prop stalagmites and termite mounds. Park and walk the boardwalk and
dip a finger, tasting: Mono Lake looks like water yet is slimy and bitter
and surprisingly frigid. In the 1950s, it was a stand-in for Krakatoa in a
bad history movie. Later, Clint Eastwood's *High Plains Drifter* was shot
here, as was the cover for Pink Floyd's *Wish You Were Here*. Scanning out
today from the crusty, bathtub-ring shoreline, one might see five hundred wild swans or a million and a half eared grebes—or maybe just a
killdeer or two and miles of empty saltiness. It depends on the month
and the state of the bloom of four trillion sea monkeys.

Go ahead, kids, try this at home. The recipe comes from the Mono
Lake Committee's website but is widely agreed to be accurate. To
make Mono Lake in your kitchen, start with a big pot. Add a gallon of
snowmelt. Heat. Now add eighteen tablespoons of baking soda, ten
tablespoons of table salt, eight tablespoons of Epsom salt, a handful of
Borax or the most caustic laundry soap you can find, and a pinch or two
of strontium, magnesium, arsenic, lithium, iodine, tungsten, and pluto-
nium. Repeat as necessary until you have enough water to cover Santa
Monica sixty feet deep.

Mark Twain was here in 1862 and wrote about it in *Roughing It*. He
had more fun having a bad time than anybody since Virgil in the *Georgics*
described all the ways a sheep can get sick and die (and there are a lot).
According to Wikipedia, Cinderella shot a video here, though they are
not my band so I report that as hearsay. If the visual cliché of the 2008

elections was a Prius at Trader Joe's with an Obama bumper sticker, in the '80s it would have been a beater truck with "Save Mono Lake" on one of its sagging bumpers. Starting in 1941, L.A.'s Department of Water and Power began drinking up all of the input creeks, which in turn (via evaporation) concentrated salts and so on, turning Mono Lake into a toxic sump. This is bad, because a native kind of shrimp and a scuba-diving fly are an essential part of migration's Big Picture. No shrimp, then no birds, simple math. Meanwhile, falling lake levels meant that the islands the snowy plovers and California gulls nested on were linked by spits to the mainland, and oh boy, the coyotes were loving it. Cue up the bumper stickers: lawsuits were started, rallies held, T-shirts sold. In the end Los Angeles had to agree to put some of the water back, maintaining a sustainable lake and moderately intact riparian corridors spidering down from Yosemite like small green gardens. The 1994 court decision secretly shocked many eco-warriors. Us'n plain folks—the little guys— won one against The Man. Right on.

Shrimp drive everything at Mono Lake, or, rather, what four or five or six trillion brine shrimp don't feed in the main lake, the edge of flies slathered along the summer shore make up for in equal balance. Even the Native Americans called themselves Fly Eaters. They harvested the pupae of Mono Lake's alkali flies in mail bag-sized reed baskets held in place by tump lines, and when the harvest was dried in the sun and hulled, it looked like mounds of yellow rice. At fifteen calories per rice grain and with an ideal balance of fat and protein, the dried fly pupae sustained indigenous populations up and down the Eastern Sierra and across into Yosemite Valley. Today, the alkali flies feed resident and migrant birds— phalaropes and gulls and avocets and Brewer's blackbirds—and as bugs go, are among the noblest flies invented since they do not bite and are indifferent to people and, in fact, scurry out of the way if you walk along the shore in late summer and take pictures of the tufa towers and smile at how the swallows loop and bank, Peaceable Kingdom from cumulous to cow patties.

The title of a very good painting by Albert Bierstadt would have been *Mono Lake by Moonlight*. Not to praise aesthetics beyond all reason, but under a full moon in winter, the place has to be the most beautiful toxic sump in America. It is worth going just for that. The whole Eastern Sierra is often heart-breakingly beautiful, especially in winter, when the mountains themselves are more snowy and sheer than any normal god would allow. Dominant plant is sagebrush, genus *Artemisia*, the name of a small press and also the center of a poem by Gary Snyder, "Earrings Dangling and Miles of Desert," in *Mountains and Rivers Without End.* In my copy of *Native American Ethnobotany*, the entries for things to do with all the varieties of Artemisia run for eleven single-spaced pages; let's just say that if everything outside of the city limits looks like a drab grey bush to you, you have 20,000 years of catching up to do.

The history of incest is the history of history because otherwise, how can we explain such screwball, inbred, goiter-necked facts as a Mono Lake, post-Indian and pre-Tioga Pass last-chance gas station, which had its own railroad (to ferry vanilla scented old-growth Jeffrey Pine to the mines of Bodie and Aurora), its own steamers (ditto, plus ore, coming back), its own fish food factory (still extant, beneath a hill north of Lee Vining), its own pumice mine (also still extant, and you pass it and the county dump and a few very recent cinder cones on the way to the South Tufa parking lot), and its own rutabaga farm? The history of the Indians killing the Indians and then the whites killing the Indians that the Indians didn't kill is nauseatingly archetypal, so we can skip over that, but I suppose we should linger on Cold War images of the U.S. Navy detonating massive underwater explosions to film the tsunamis coming ashore, just to figure out what an atom bomb does, exactly. The barracks are gone but there is an S.S. Minnow white propeller and a bronze plaque on the dirt road that leads down to the place where you put in kayaks, still called today Navy Beach. One wants it to make sense, yet somehow visit after visit, it never quite does. Cf. Anne Carson: "Anthropology is a science of mutual surprise."

Anne Carson said too, "We live by waters breaking out of the heart." This comes from *Plainwater*, via "The Anthropology of Water." She was talking about me, about a time when I was a new stepdad and I took the kids to Mono Lake. We stayed in a motel and went hiking and found the weathered hull of a plank boat overturned in the brush. In the pictures the boys are wearing my Patagonia gloves, which is odd because they kept losing them, two or three pair a day, so as I recall, by that day of the trip everybody was out of gloves, and also hats, extra sweaters, and clean underwear. I was in love with their mother the way a volcano loves the sky and so is always surprised when the great photogenic arcs of magma suddenly hit the glass ceiling of gravity and splash back down defeated on the sides of the fissure. I mean this not as sexual reference but in the sense that hardening into asphalt is a surprise for anybody.

Geography is memory in three ways. One is that you will always be disappointed with Paris or the Sahara since to go at all to a place, not only do they speak French, but first you learned about it from National Geographic television specials or a chapter in school, so the reality will never be as good as cinematography's promises. Two is that after you go, you can replay the scenes and make them better. Even if you hated it, your hatred perfects itself. Three is that places make no sense if we are honest and listen to the broken water of our hearts. Instead of objective geography, place means the place where you got a speeding ticket or heard a kind of bird that sounded like bent wire or first learned that if you kiss with your tongue you probably should first wear rubber-soled shoes and other non-conductive clothing. I am sorry that Mono Lake is now a National Scenic Postcard Area, sorry that people now know, because it was just mine first—a discarded, dirt-road kind of place to sleep in my truck on climbing trips, waking up in a North Face down bag facing the tufa domes where the South Parking Lot is now (no camping allowed, $3 per person entrance fee), a place that glowed numinously as the sun came up and I peed in the sagebrush and every thing in my body, my world, my horizon was alive with possibility. Later this place became something more necessary and even more holy, a pilgrimage site (and still an illegal camping stop) as I made the Hank Williams drive from L.A. to Bridgeport or Reno on visitation weekends to pick up my daughter whose mom, like an errant comet, lived her life in parabolas. I needed the centering it gave me, not so much beauty as the certainty that I could do this, it would be all right, I could keep my temper and write the checks and make the drives and above all find the small happy place in the world for my daughter and me to exist as a family. An odd family, to be sure, as odd as the towers of South Tufa made out of spackle and toothpaste, but a family, dammit, now and forever. There is something about the way some kinds of light come to you that is indelible and sustaining, not as in an abstract word like faith but as a hard, real thing, light that pushes

you back on your feet or goes into your eyes through your ribs. There are
some very good, artistically satisfying photographs of Mono Lake (Galen
Rowell, et al.) but as with photographs of Notre Dame or the Sahara,
they are Other to the reality of what you will remember yourself if you
go to Mono Lake or maybe if you have been or if the State of California
says you may see your children on alternate Saturdays and once extra at
Christmas. Our bodies inhabit reality not in the present but in the fog
and brushfire of expectation and memory, so that Mono Lake can mean
a bumper sticker and Mark Twain even as it also can mean that the ducks
look like trash out past that little island and that once, in East Africa, a
British guide was fast-forwarding through bird tapes he had recorded in
America, and he happened to stop on a sweet, churring *wheeurr*, which is
the song of a Sage Thrasher, and it takes you directly back to a time when
you slept in your truck one March morning at Mono Lake, and how when
you woke up a Sage Thrasher was teed-up on the eldest, most six-foot-
tall sage, singing a song just like that, and there you were, in Africa yet
about to cry you were smiling so hard with happiness and the burning
incandescence of memory. ✑

2017 Finalist

Lawrence Lenhart

PROJECT DESCRIPTION

Note: Lawrence Lenhart's original proposal was titled Rewilding the Ferret. The writing sample that follows is an updated section of the proposed book.

Focusing on four sites in Arizona's high desert, *Rewilding the Ferret* tells the story of conservation against the backdrop of the Sixth Mass Extinction, spanning the desert regions between the U.S.-Mexico Border and the Grand Canyon. I've written essays about nocturnal spotlighting events, land use cooperation, and captive breeding technologies. The remaining chapters will be about Mexican cartel interference with conservation in Chihuahua, a pilgrimage to the oldest fossil remains of the species in the Great Basin Desert (Nevada), and the "micro" deserts of the American West, particularly near Dinétah in the Painted Desert. I will shadow and interview ranchers and wildlife specialists, and continue to spotlight Arizonan ranchlands.

The majority of the fieldwork will be in the semiarid grasslands and sage-steppe of the Colorado Plateau, with other chapters set in northern Mexico, southern Arizona, and Nevada. *Rewilding the Ferret* draws on works such as *Hope is a Thing With Feathers* (Cokinos); *Eating Stone: Imagination and the Loss of the Wild* (Meloy); *Killing the Hidden Waters* (Bowden); *The Deep Zoo* (Ducornet); *Zoologies* (Deming); and the research and writing of sociobiologist Edward O. Wilson.

Whereas some essayists have succumbed to what Deming has called "ceaseless elegy," my essay will celebrate the ferret's return from the brink, and the human intervention that keeps it that way. In this book, the desert will be a place where biophilia reigns and where human activity can be equally ruinous and restorative. Desert ecologists have long debated whether the Colorado Plateau qualifies as a desert. Because I am interested in the effects of anthropogenic activity on desert ecologies, the book will make the provocative case that the plateau is fast becoming a desert due to overgrazing and prairie dog eradication. By the end of this book, it will seem as if the ferret exists to coax humans into having more nuanced, dynamic, and propulsive conversations about the desert.

My Son Was Born to Rob Me
of the Glory of Saving the Black-Footed Ferret

WHEN THE NURSERY IS READY enough, I shimmy a tent into the back of my car, plus a notebook, some reading, and a change of clothes. I swerve off the Williams exit toward the kitschy Grand Canyon corridor on AZ-64. My wife is on the hands-free for as long as reception will allow for it. We debate which would be a worse fate for me: missing the birth of our firstborn or contracting the plague. It is not a theoretical question—nor, as my wife points out, are these options mutually exclusive.

"It doesn't matter. They could both happen to you tonight," she says through the Braxton Hicks contractions, which the books describe as a kind of crampy false labor.

They're just about the last words I hear before the call drops. I drive past Grand Canyon Junction, past Joe's Route 66 Hot Dogs, and past the gates to the Big "D" Ranch. Just before Red Lake Valley, I see the sign for Espee Road. In just one month's time, an article in the *Williams News* will open: "After fleas tested positive for plague last month near the Red Lake area north of Williams…" The Espee range is dew-dropped and tangy with manure. As promised by an Arizona Game and Fish email, I cross a cattle guard at 27.8 miles. Before getting out of the car to open the first gate, I stuff the cuffs of my pants into my wool socks. Like the long-sleeve shirt, cotton-latex gloves, and bug spray, it's a form of insurance against the fleas. I have been reading about plague all week as if I'm a casual scholar and not some neurotic game-and-fish volunteer.

The basics: A pathogen is carried by a vector to the vertebrate host, which is then stricken with the disease. E.g., The bacterium *Yersinia pestis* is carried by a flea to a prairie dog, which comes down with the bubonic plague.

As for humans, I made the mistake of sharing *this* description from the Minnesota Department of Health with my wife: "people get bubonic plague from infected animals. The bacteria are spread by bites from infected fleas, bites or scratches from infected animals, or direct contact with infected animal carcasses."

"And what is it that you're going to be doing at Espee Ranch?" she asked me, leadingly.

"Volunteering."

She rolled her eyes, so I tried again.

"Saving ferrets."

The more truthful version goes like this: "I'm trapping known verte-brate hosts, knocking them out with anesthesia, taking blood samples, and combing vectors off their backs to send to the CDC who will check for evidence of the pathogen, which is responsible for one of the deadli-est diseases in human history."

She knows I'm not some tedious thrill-seeker like her ex was, just a sucker for the black-footed ferret, the endangered species whose exis-tence in northern Arizona is entirely dependent on the health of the prairie dog population. Senior Biologist of the World Wildlife Fund Kristy Bly has called the prairie dog the McNugget of the prairie. In fact, she and colleagues in Montana oversee an operation in which: "Pilots fly [drones] across the prairie, dropping blueberry-sized pellets about every 30 feet. They are flavored to taste like peanut butter... The kicker is that they're laced with a live vaccine that protects [prairie dogs] from the plague." They have even shot vaccine-coated M&M's onto the prairie from their airborne apparatus, which has been likened to a "glorified gumball machine." "Save the food and you save the ferret," the article reckons. It's a logical wager. This is why I don't hesitate to lend a hand despite warnings from administrators, through national megaphones like *USA Today* and ABC, to stay away. "Officials are urging residents to reduce their exposure to the disease," one outlet says over a satellite map of *my* residential area.

That, and the black-footed ferret has always been more auspice than omen for me. Over the years, the volunteering has always aligned with important moments in my personal history—as if it was my own spiri-tual existence, and not the ferret's biological one, that was at stake.

We made sure one of her closest friends was available in case she went into labor, and now here I am, rolling up to the primitive camp: a small village of tired trucks parked in a dirt roundabout, stacks of rusting cages under a canopy, a kitchen with locked coolers and a gas stove, and a semicircle of REI tents raised in the limited shade of the piñon-juniper woodland.

I spritz my torso with too much bug spray. By the time I cover my forehead, ear, neck, shirt, sleeves, wrists, palms, fingers, and thumbs, I've run out of the elixir completely. It's just a rustic campsite, momentarily abandoned. I stick my finger into the water, still hot from a recent boil, and realize I must have just missed them. Breakfast too.

"Oh good, you found us!" Jennifer says when the conservation team has returned to the camp.

I greet her with a thumbs-up, emerging from my tent, toothbrush poking out of my mouth.

"I just got a voicemail from one of the other volunteers. They made a wrong turn and just went home."

"You have reception out here?" I ask. I wonder if my wife still has Jennifer's number from our last spotlighting trip, if she'll think to use it in case of membrane rupture (water breakage).

"Kind of," she says while squinting at her phone's screen. "Well, no." She explains they were just on an ice run back to Red Valley. Behind her, interns pour the ice bag into the cooler while others crouch at the wheel well of a truck.

"We'll get going in a little bit," Jennifer says. "When it cools down."

Because one of the trucks was clogged with brush the day before and an engine spark started a little fire in the undercarriage, we're down to three trucks to attend to four sites. It's sunset, and I want to know how the intern at the wheel knows where she's going. She's only been on this nondescript farm road once before, and she makes masterful hairpin turns without consulting map or GPS.

"This next turn," she says, "I know because there's a burrowing owl just chilling."

Sure enough, when the truck turns again, wide this time like a jibing sailboat, I'm rubbernecking at an owl who stands on its twiggy legs at a steep entrance mound. While burrowing owls and black-footed ferrets are both squatters in the prairie dog's colony, at least the owl is courteous enough not to devour its landlord. Due to the suspicion of plague, there is an uneasy fear among state conservationists that a ferret's next meal will be its last. The inter-colony transmission of plague could be instantly fatal for any living specimens associated with the black-footed ferret project in northern Arizona, which in 2017, peaked at a minimum population of just nineteen.

The site is marked by a lollipop reflector. The traps are arranged all across the field, and the sun glints off their west-facing aluminum walls. We slalom the rows, giving each spring-loaded trapdoor a swift high-five so that they catch on the treadle latch. We add a couple cotton balls for nesting and cast a spoonful of oats, millet, and kibble just beyond the treadle, enough to lure small Rodentia. After the Sherman traps, we switch to the larger Tomahawks with steel wire frames. These are for the prairie dogs. We double the bait on their treadles, and converge on the truck again. Each of us gulps some of the water stored in the truck bed before dropping to our haunches. We sit, silent, privately trying to process the sun's slippage through the broad horizon, the way the clouds bear the weight of all that color until they don't.

Dinner happens so quickly—the prepping, chowing, cleaning—that it feels like the spaghetti is coiled inside my gut, balled up like one large noodle. Since we'll wake at 4 AM, we hurry to the tents and try for sleep. I unroll my socks and crack my toe knuckles, flick the lantern off and slip into my scalloped sleeping bag.

Unable to sleep, though, I creep away under a filmy moon glow, taking a spotlight with me. In the unlikely case of a black-footed ferret's green eye shine. I haven't been sleeping for the past week thanks to my wife's tossing on the mattress. Her back pain, along with the Braxton Hicks contractions, have rendered her sleepless as well. She even pointed out that I'd probably sleep better in my tent tonight than I have on our memory foam mattress.

I walk for twenty minutes—no more than a mile—swinging my spotlight over prairie dog entrance mounds and desperately hoping my phone will vibrate.

NO BABY YET

or

THE BABY'S HERE. COME QUICK!

or

YOU ASSHOLE

Anything will do. By the time I've returned to the camp, the others' have woken to their alarms. Not even dawn, and it's time to check the traps. After a mug of instant coffee, I'm in the truck with the interns again. This time, we relish the silence. The burrowing owl is burrowed. A weak flash of blue urges in from the east.

We stalk the rows, calling out when we've got one. A few of the smaller traps have clapped shut without an animal. It's obvious, though, when a prairie dog has been captured. It stares through the cage—either with vengeance or dismay—and we hoist it carefully to the truck. We escort the live cargo to a midway point where Jennifer and Heather set up the canopy. Equidistant from all four sites, another truck has arrived and is already processing the first grasshopper mouse.

Her eyes are two jumbo caviar, black and glassy, popping at its captor's nerve. A man has dumped the mouse into a transparent wholesale pretzel jar and is now clasping a mesh tea ball infuser around a cotton ball that's been doused in general anesthetic. Once the ball has rolled to the base of the container, the lid is screwed on and we wait. Immediately, the rodent staggers. Onlookers compare him to a punch-drunk boxer, a last-call boozer, a cartoonish dental patient. I try to laugh, but nothing comes out. Eventually, the mouse drops. They rattle the container and nothing changes. In the man's gloved hands, the limp mouse looks bitesize, a little bigger than a marshmallow Peep. We pay close attention as its toenail is snipped, and blood is collected in a vial.

"If we don't get blood from the nail, we can yank a whisker too," Heather says.

As she brushes its back with a toothbrush, hoping to loose some fleas into a small basin on the folding table, the mouse comes back to life. The man, who has been using one hand to scruff the mouse in the event it regains consciousness, alerts the crew. Someone tilts the pretzel jar his way, and just like that, the mouse is anesthetized once again. A few minutes after the processing, she is back in the Sherman trap, ready to be returned to the exact spot she ate her last meal.

Once the samples are labeled, it's our team's turn to process a kangaroo rat. We repeat the procedure, each person taking on the role they're most comfortable with. Next up: another kangaroo rat. And another. When one of the interns spills the next grasshopper mouse out of the container, though, it sails past his palm and ricochets off the tabletop. It's unconscious, concussed. Again, the crew resorts to caricature, treating the incident like a groin hit on *America's Funniest Home Videos*. Its fur is combed for fleas (two!) and blood is drawn. Then it's returned to its cage and casket. After that, everyone's a little more careful.

The procedure is a little different for the prairie dog, most of it relating to scale. A larger container, more isoflurane, a longer wait time until paralysis. The biggest difference, though, is the scruffing technique and this warning: "Now, don't let these guys nip you. Their teeth are a whole other story." A prairie dog's cheek teeth grow continuously. It's only through constant gnawing (i.e., filing) that they don't drag their teeth on the ground with them everywhere they go.

As the first prairie dogs are processed—energetic juveniles who scramble against the walls of the container, trying to burrow their way out—I can't help but recall the Department of Health's explanation: "People get bubonic plague from... bites or scratches from infected animals." I squint at them. *Are you infected?* Are you? Once they faint, these dogs are dumped and scruffed, snipped and combed, and returned to the Tomahawks from which they came.

When it's my turn to scruff the prairie dog, it's a very large adult who weighs in at a jumbo two-and-a-half pounds; in other words, he's maxed out. The specialists give him the same amount of anesthesia as the others, which concerns me, but they have procedures to follow. After a drawn-out wobble around the circumference of the container, the dog finally drops. I grip him like my life depends on it, like it's the 'hold-my-hand' cliff moment in the penultimate scene of an action movie. When he thrashes back to life not twenty seconds later, I tell the person on containment duty he's going back in.

We all stare at the prairie dog in the jar. No one dares to make fun of this one. If someone will be scratched or bitten today, here's the likely perpetrator. The anesthesia process is repeated, and perhaps we all look the other way when Heather gives the cotton ball an extra splash. This time, when the animal slumps against the wall, gravity pinning him in place, we're all convinced of his slumber.

Turns out medical grade nitrile disposable gloves—famous for their flexibility, dexterity, and "dependable barrier protection"—were not designed to defend against the canines of a two-and-a-half pound, agitated prairie dog. When he tosses back to life, he slips from my right hand. It's the left hand, swinging to support the prairie dog's torso, that sustains the bite which punctures the glove. The dog returns to the container, a flimsy holding cell, while I fling the glove off. The skin appears to be contused, not abraded. I'm the recipient of rapid concern and antiseptic, but I look beyond my finger as Jennifer and Heather quickly paint the prairie dog's blood on Nobuto sample strips. I remember the gist of Jennifer's ambiguous email a couple weeks back: "There is a possibility that there is plague at one of our trapping sites."

The animals are unceremoniously returned to the easting and northing from where we plucked them up. After that, I leave in a hurry. My tent is stuffed, not folded, into the canvas bag; after going through the motions of being a team member—inventorying cages, lifting canteens, exchanging emails with the new interns—I am waving goodbye, my injured hand the last they see of me.

I close the gate on the Babbitt allotment, knowing I am leaving this tract, this project, behind for a short while.

The way I see it: If twenty years from now my son wants to know why I missed his birth, I'll simply tell him: *This other thing, this ferret thing, that was important also.* A friend jokes that maybe he'll return the favor by ditching my funeral.

I pass windmills and watch their blades chop the sky. By now, I'm checking my phone every 0.8 miles or something like that, waiting for the first trace of a signal. I know this will probably be my last time in the field for a while. The bite mark is gnashed into my flesh. It's still possible that I've missed the birth of my son *and* that I've contracted plague. *I was meant to be a volunteer, not a martyr,* I think. It's possible too that the black-footed ferrets are the next in line, that this is their last summer ever in Arizona.

My pocket buzzes. The brakes squawk. A dust cloud of my own making drifts over me. I listen to my wife's voicemail and speed homeward.

2016 Winner

Tara FitzGerald

PROJECT DESCRIPTION

"No Water of Their Own," focuses on the desertification of Central Asia's Aral Sea, addressing what happens when a sea becomes a desert, and when a sea people, therefore, become desert people. My project also plans to explore what will happen to the desert formed on the desiccated sea bed if the sea does come back.

As recently as the 1960s, the Aral Sea was the fourth largest inland body of water in the world. Its cobalt expanse lay deep inside the sprawling territory of the Soviet Union and, with a surface area of 26,061 square miles, it was just a tad larger than the state of West Virginia. Then, in the 1960s, the Soviet authorities decided to expand their cotton industry, which had its base in Central Asia. As cotton is a very thirsty crop, they ordered an expansion of their sprawling network of irrigation canals, gradually siphoning more and more water away from the Aral Sea. And over the last fifty years, as the sea dried up and the fish disappeared, a desert formed in the spaces where the waves used to break.

In recent years, catfish, bream, carp, pike-perch and other fish have reappeared in part of the Aral Sea and, in the fishing villages near Aralsk, fishermen are once again taking to their boats and going fishing. In 2005, a dam built on the sea allowed water levels on the Kazakh side to rise, salinity levels to drop, and the sea to creep closer to the port once again. In the last five years, several new fish processing plants have appeared in the town of Aralsk, and some 600 fishermen are now licensed to fish in the Aral Sea.

All this poses some important questions: Is it truly possible to reverse such dramatic environmental change as the disappearance of a sea? And what will happen to the desert formed upon the desiccated seabed if the sea does come back?

No Water of Their Own

[B]eyond the city, up to the horizon, we saw the dead craters
of harsh moon ash on the endless plain where the sea had
been.

—Gabriel Garcia Marquez,
The Autumn of the Patriarch (1975)

ONCE THERE WAS A MAN WHO had a hole in his heart the size of
the sea, and nothing but the sea could fill it. He had waited many years
for the faithless waves to return. In fact, that's all he had done since the
moment he realized the waters were retreating from his shores and the
land was turning to a desert before his eyes. In the intervening decades,
his wife had died and his children had moved away from that place. And
still he waited. But the sea never came, and the desert continued to grow.

"This is a town of ghosts now," his son told him, encouraging him to
pack up and leave. Sailo nodded. It was. But he couldn't imagine living
anywhere else.

And so he sat, day in and day out, on a lumpy, stained mattress up on
a bluff in the former port of Moynaq, staring out across the desiccated
landscape, his dark eyes squinting against the dust and wind. Maybe it
was hope, or maybe it was despair. Either way, he didn't seem to know or
even to care any more. The vigil itself had become his reason for living.
In the sand below him, where the harbor used to be, was the so-called
graveyard of ships—a place where skeletal vessels lay marooned on sand
dunes, also waiting for a sea that never came. The rusting hulks of twelve
boats covered in graffiti scribbles, varying in size from small six-foot tugs
to barges up to twenty feet long, were the remains of what had once been
a thriving maritime and fishing industry in former Soviet Uzbekistan.

On a July day in 2011 I found Sailo there, as was his custom, smoking a cigarette. His face was more lines than not, his eyes watery and blood-shot, and his sunken cheeks gave him something of the appearance of a ghost himself. He had just a few yellowed teeth left clinging to his gums, and a relief pattern of thin, raised scars crisscrossed his bare, concave chest. He wore a pair of ragged grey trousers, held up by a piece of string, and his feet were swathed in plastic sandals.

It was only 8 A.M. in the now-defunct port town, and the temperature had already reached 115 degrees. Two fat beads of sweat crawled steadily down my body like beetles, one weaving drunkenly along the gulley of my spine and the other making a slow, ticklish descent of my chest. I plucked at the hem of my rust-colored cotton t-shirt to dislodge the drops of per-spiration and the material bloomed darker in patches as it fell back and stuck to my skin. Gazing out over the desert scene before me, it seemed almost impossible to believe that just fifty years ago the white-crested waves of the Aral Sea used to break over the top of the bluff where I was standing. Now, there was not a single drop of water to be seen.

The Aral Sea was once the fourth largest inland body of water in the world. As recently as the 1960s, it boasted a surface area of 26,061 square miles—making it a just a tad larger than the state of West Virginia. The sea's cobalt expanse lay at the heart of the Soviet Central Asian landmass, straddling the border between what are now the inde-pendent states of Kazakhstan and Uzbekistan, and it was surpassed in size only by the nearby Caspian Sea, Lake Superior in North America and Lake Victoria in Africa. The majestic Amu Darya and Syr Darya rivers—famed as the Oxus and Jaxartes of antiquity and once traversed with great difficulty by Alexander the Great—traveled more than three thou-sand miles between them to replenish the sea with fresh water.

Central Asia is a vast tract of land that occupies the southernmost rump of what was once the Soviet Union. Its area is almost half that of the mainland United States, and it shares a border to the north and northeast with Russia. China lies to its southeast, while Iran and Afghanistan mark the limits of its territory to the south. Its western border is formed by the Caspian Sea. After the collapse of the Soviet Union in 1991, Central Asia split into five separate countries, sometimes colloquially referred to as the "Stans." Kazakhstan, at almost four times the size of Texas, accounts for the bulk of this territory and covers its entire northern flank, while Turkmenistan, Uzbekistan, Tajikistan, and Kyrgyzstan cluster below it, west to east, in that order.

For most of the twentieth century, the Stans were hidden away in a zone of the Soviet Union that was largely closed to foreigners. They were some of the USSR's most desolate and neglected republics, as well as one of Moscow's dumping grounds for agricultural experiments, political undesirables, nuclear testing, and bio-weapons storage—anything the Soviet government didn't want too close to home.

It was also during the Soviet era—in the 1930s and 1940s—that the two fishing towns at each end of the Aral Sea developed into major fishing ports: Aral to the north on the Kazakh side, and Moynaq to the south on the Uzbek side. They thrummed with the activities of fishermen and boat builders, the busy production lines of the state-owned fish canneries, incoming and outgoing passenger steamers, cargo ships and fishing trawlers, and hordes of holidaymakers from the Soviet elite arriving in search of sun, sand and sea.

I squatted down beside Sailo and asked him, with the help of my young Uzbek translator, what the town of Moynaq had been like when he was a young man. He told me he was fifty-seven, but he looked at least a decade older. Back then, he said, the harbor buzzed with life early each morning. In the feeble dawn light gulls dived and swooped above the boats, crying out to each other in their guttural voices, scavenging for food. The waves slapped against the edges of the bluff and the chains of the anchors clanked, metal on metal, against the boats that bobbed in the water. In different voices, still husky with sleep, the men of the fishing brigades called out greetings to their comrades, pulled on their waterproofs, shook out their nets, prepared to start their day.

Throughout his teenage years in the late 1960s, Sailo worked as a boat captain on various large fishing vessels based in Moynaq, including the Lebed, which lay rusting in the sand below us. Each day he would skilfully navigate the waves and ferry his brigade of six fishermen out to the Aral Sea's prime fishing locations. When the men returned in the afternoons with their haul of fish—pike, carp, maybe sturgeon if they were lucky—they would unload them onto the docks. Most of the catch went directly to the state canning factory across the way, but some was set aside to take to the drying house for salting and smoking. Then the men could sit back and smoke cigarettes, play cards, swallow down rounds of beer or vodka, and chew on dried fish.

But when Sailo returned from completing his two years of compulsory military service with the Red Army in the early 1970s, things had already begun to change for the worse in Moynaq. It was then that his beloved sea started to slip away, taking his livelihood as a boat captain with it.

Driving toward Moynaq earlier that same day, along a raised strip of land and over a bridge where no water flowed anymore, I could see how the port used to sit on an isthmus. A sign declared MOYNAQ in bold red letters, and beneath it were two undulating lines—white above blue—like the stylized waves you might see in a child's drawing. But to see the waters that once washed the edges of this port, and begin to understand the true extent of the sea's decline, requires a bone-rattling, three-hour drive in a 4x4 jeep across the dry, cracked former seabed (now the desert) in pursuit of its retreating shoreline. The edge of the Aral Sea now lies around one hundred miles from Moynaq's harbor. The distance from New York City to Philadelphia.

In preparation for my trip I had looked up the Aral Sea in my 2003 atlas, the most up-to-date version I owned. Less than accurately, it still showed the sea as one large body of water, an intact baby-blue blob. In fact, the sea had split into two distinct parts sometime in the 1980s. It seemed strange that the rapid shrinking of such a huge geographical feature, and the formation of the world's youngest desert (the Aralkum) in its wake, had not been recorded in those pages. It was almost as if it had never happened.

In more recent NASA satellite photos, the sea glowed like a greenish-blue jewel wedged between the dusty browns of Central Asia's more established deserts—the Karakum ('black sand') and the Kyzylkum ('red sand'). In these pictures it was clear that the Aral was no longer one sea, but had instead separated into a northern and a southern mass, with a strip of land cutting a horizontal swath between them. Between the sea and its original shoreline ran a shadowy grey band—like the halo shimmer on an overexposed photograph. It was just a sliver in some places and a substantial slab in others; a ghostly image of the waters that no longer flowed there. A desert forming as a photo negative of the sea.

Sailo recalled the days when the harbor was jammed full of boats loaded down with fish or salt. When yurts—traditional nomadic tents with domed wooden frameworks draped in felt—and restaurants selling dried fish snacks and beer used to line the now-empty promenade. When the seafront bustled with tourists and locals strolling in the sunshine, taking in the sea air and paddling in the Aral's temperate waters. When I visited, the town's tiny airport—which once buzzed with the comings and goings of weekend holidaymakers—was a dilapidated shell of a building, filled only with empty beer bottles, broken glass, and cigarette butts.

Sailo said the fish from the Aral had been famed as the tastiest in all of the Soviet Union. Then he brushed roughly at his brimming eyes and turned away from me to light another cigarette. "Oh and the Aral caviar," he added, his eyes lighting up again briefly. Black caviar from the Aral sturgeon was plentiful and valuable back then. But he hadn't seen any in years.

I climbed down the twenty metal steps at the edge of the bluff to examine the ship corpses. There was no one else around. No one else had been foolish enough to make the trip there that day in the July heat. The air lower down was heavy, stultifying, and I felt light-headed, leaning against the sun-baked metal for support. I looked up at the wall several meters above me and imagined the weight of the water-that-was pressing down upon me.

Across the main road from the harbor, I came across an abandoned fish cannery. The graveyard of ships lay on one side of the main road and the fish cannery directly across from it on the other, bookends to the port's decline. At its entrance stood a pale blue billboard painted in the Socialist Realist style of Soviet propaganda posters. Two strong-featured fishermen in orange boots and wet gear hauled in a net full of leaping fish, while behind them a female factory worker in a white coat and an orange headscarf gestured toward the many boxes of fish piled high beside her.

"Glory To Labor!" the painted slogan running across the top of the main building still declared, although it was faded now.

In a black-and-white snapshot from the 1950s that I had examined earlier in the Moynaq town museum, workers dressed in white coats and hats sorted through mounds of fish piled high on the cannery production lines. In another old photo, rows and rows of cannery workers decked out in their Sunday finery attended a special concert put on for them by the management to encourage a sense of community.

If the Aral once supplied the port's lifeblood, then the cannery was its beating heart. At its height throughout the 1940s, '50s and '60s, Moynaq's cannery produced tens of millions of cans of fish every year. Now, its buildings were carcasses split open to the elements, rotting in the unrelenting heat, their stripped concrete bones reaching for the sun. The cloudless sky glimmered azure through gashes in the bricks, and children scrabbled for treasure among discarded bits of cardboard and plastic. In another corner, a group of men lounged in deckchairs, some dozing and others playing cards or smoking—construction workers on a lunchtime break.

A tall, gaunt man with hollow cheeks, dressed in a button-down shirt, loose pants, and a flat cap, offered to show me around the cannery ruins. He told me he had worked there for thirty years. He had tended the furnaces where the fish were cooked, until the factory was finally shut down twenty years ago. Production had been cut in half as fish supplies dwindled through the 1970s and '80s, but the lines were kept running by importing frozen fish from other parts of the Soviet Union—from Russia and the Baltic states of Estonia, Latvia, and Lithuania. But after the USSR collapsed in 1991 and the various republics went their separate ways, Moynaq's cannery was left to fend for itself. He pointed to where the refrigeration unit had stood, the building where the fish were skinned and de-boned, and the canteen where the workers ate together.

"That's where we used to have lunch every day," he said. My eyes followed to where his hand indicated some tall metal struts with only a handful of bricks still cleaving to them. "It makes me want to weep seeing it like this."

I left the cannery and walked back along the main road, a dusty and seemingly infinite stretch of tarmac. At the graveyard in the middle of town, I peered through a gap between the bright blue metal gates and saw clusters of Russian Orthodox crosses, some made out of metal and others of wood. They looked a little like outdoor television antennae—a vertical bar with a small, horizontal crosspiece placed near the top, followed by a longer one just below it, and finally a slanted crossbar close to the base. *Gorodskoye Kladbishchye No. 1,* the sign read in Russian. Town Cemetery No. 1. Evidence of the sizeable Russian community that once lived here.

Outside the padlocked gates of the cemetery I talked to Yevgeny, one of just a handful of ethnic Russians still left in Moynaq. He punctuated his speech with a melancholy refrain. *"Uyekhal,"* he kept saying, as he talked about the sea, *"Uyekhal."* The sea left, and it left, and it left. Although he was well into his seventies, his dark, wavy hair showed barely a trace of gray. He wore it combed carefully to one side in a style reminiscent of a 1930s movie star, and the skin on his face was tanned to a deep chestnut brown. At first the sea slipped away slowly, he explained, but then it began to flee faster and faster from its shores. In my head, this scene played out like accelerating time-lapse photography. *"Zdyes nichevo nyet,"* he said. "There's nothing left here now."

A huge number of families had called it quits, and packed up and left a long time ago, when it became clear that the economy had all but disappeared along with the sea. Of those that remained, it was often only the mothers, or grandparents, and children that still lived in Moynaq, while most of the menfolk had headed north across the border into Kazakhstan to seek work, legally or illegally.

As I walked along the edge of the empty street, I kicked up dust, my mouth and eyes already itchy with it. Herds of skinny cows and an occasional stray dog roamed around, but it was rare to see another human being. Official figures put the population of the former port at around thirteen thousand, but the unofficial word on the street is that it's more like eight or nine thousand—less than ten percent of what it was fifty years ago.

A dusty collection of beach balls and a plastic bucket and spade hung outside a small shop. These seaside toys seemed mocking, disorienting somehow. A sudden movement caught my eye. I turned and watched a small boy bend down to poke at something moving in the dirt. It was a seagull with one of its wings almost entirely sheared off, the bloody gash already crusty from dragging in the sand.

In order to go in search of what remained of the Aral Sea, I left Moynaq behind me and headed due north, towards the border with Kazakhstan. The GPS clipped to the dashboard of the Russian-made jeep I was rattling along in showed a splotch of cornflower blue at the top of its screen. Despite continued reassurances from the driver and my translator, a young woman who was home from university for the summer vacation, we'd been driving non-stop for a couple of hours and I still hadn't seen any hint of water.

Instead, it was desert. At first, there were lines and lines of electricity pylons forming a metallic army patrolling along either side of the dirt road. Then they gave way to sparse clumps of spiky green bush poking through the cracked earth, nature reclaiming the land where the sea once flowed. Occasionally a sudden gust of wind picked up fistfuls of sand, salt, and dust and flung them at the car, engulfing us in a murky cloud and filling my mouth with grit when I didn't roll the window up fast enough.

The off-white of the sky melded with the off-white of the salt-encrusted land, blurring the line where earth left off and air began, until a huge grey landmass—the Ustyurt Plateau—loomed ahead of us. We twisted up its sheer side along a rutted track, leaning sharply into the narrow turns. And, as we rounded the final bend and reached the flat top of the plateau, suddenly the sea appeared—an intense slick of cerulean brush-stroked across the horizon, as if by a giant invisible hand.

From that vantage point it looked static and unreal, almost too vivid. Stretching before the sea was a lumpy, lunar landscape, where dunes that once dwelled below the waves now lay naked and exposed.

The beach was deserted. Just the rusty bed of a large fishing trawler lay stranded at the edge of the water, the point where sand, salt, and crushed up shells gave way to thick, black mud. I slipped off my shorts and flip-flops and waded into the waves dressed only in a swimsuit and t-shirt, each step requiring an effort to extract myself from the sucking sliminess underfoot. The heavy, salty water tingled and prickled my skin—a delicious, gentle pain, like chili on the taste buds. Once it reached halfway up my thighs, I lay back and watched my mud-spattered feet emerge from the water in front of me, the sea's now-elevated salt content effortlessly cradling me afloat. There were no fish, or plants, or any other living things visible in the tepid waves.

My translator paddled at the edge of the water, while further down the beach our driver filled plastic Coke bottles with 'Aral water' to bring home.

The edges of the sky began to blur and the afternoon turned slowly into dusk. After we had set up camp on an area of high ground overlooking the sea, the three of us shared a meal of *demleme*—a stew of carrots, potatoes, and lettuce, boiled and then slow steamed in a metal pot over the campfire. We rounded off the meal with thick, sticky slices of watermelon, accompanied by a *digestif* of several vodkas. "It's medicinal," the driver said. "To clear the dust from your lungs."

My hope was that it would also act as an aid to sleep. That night we would be camping in flimsy little tents and he had just mentioned, without undue concern, that the last time he had been here he saw wolves up on the plateau. A half-remembered image from some childhood book—an ominous lupine silhouette, head tilted back, jaws open and howling at the moon—crept to mind. I kept thinking I could see wolf-like shadows prowling up there above us, waiting patiently for us to drop off to sleep.

Then the sun began to sink languidly below the horizon, tingeing the Aral Sea pink around the edges, and for a while I forgot about everything else. In its place there appeared a low-hanging full moon, an orange globe cobwebbed across by wispy, dark clouds. It trailed a chain of reflected orange moons across the flat, inky-black water behind it. We raised our glasses and drank a toast to the ailing sea: "Long live the Aral!" And also the Aralkum, I whispered to myself. ⌁

2016 Finalist

Kenneth Garcia

PROJECT DESCRIPTION

"The House of Radiant Colors: A Memoir," one chapter of a larger memoir, describes my experience working for a mining exploration company in northeastern Nevada during my late teens, where I worked alongside a geologist who sees no beauty in the natural world. (Note: This essay was first published in *Hunger Mountain,* Spring 2015.) For the geologist, the land is worthless apart from the precious metals that can be extracted from it. And yet, he knows the deep geological history of the place. This leads me to ask, how could someone who knew the deep history of this land not see beauty in it?

The memoir describes the events and experiences through which that enigmatic something becomes evermore explicit as I grow older, leading me toward a strong sense of the spiritual depths of nature—of nature as a conduit for the Holy.

The memoir also will describe an inner dialogue between the beauty and uniqueness of the Great Basin with the assumption of many casual passers-through of its uselessness and ugliness, or its purely utilitarian value of extracting minerals and depositing nuclear wastes—wastes that will remain for millennia.

I will drive to the following sites: the Oquirrh Mountains near Toole, Utah, the site of a small mining operation in the early twentieth century where I spent a summer working for a mining company in my late teens; Jarbidge, Nevada (pop. 107) along the Nevada-Idaho border; the Carlin and Bootstrap gold mines in Northeastern Nevada to witness and describe the extent of destruction since I explored the land there over thirty years ago; the ghost towns of Rawhide, Rhyolite, Goldfield, and Ionia; the Great Basin National Park to visit the ancient Bristlecone Pine trees, some of which live almost 5,000 years in spite of dry, harsh desert conditions; and alkalai flats, or playas, which abound in the Great Basin.

The Hollow Places of the World

THIS CHAPTER DESCRIBES the very beginning phase of a spiritual awakening in the outback of Nevada, and so I begin with an epigraph from St. Augustine:

The ores of divine providence
are everywhere infused, and
everywhere to be found.

The margins of the world surrounded me—at least in the physical sense—for hundreds of miles in every direction: a no-man's land of semi-arid deserts; middles of nowhere; and solitary mountain ranges. I lived in this no-man's land, in the small town of Elko, Nevada, and worked in its middles of nowhere during the last two years of high school and the first two of college. I spent summers searching for gold in the remote mountains and hills of Nevada, assisting geologists from Newmont Exploration Company. We hiked rocky hillsides covered with gnarled brush and pungent with the smell of juniper and sage. We scoured long-abandoned mining towns and uninhabited landscapes searching for hidden traces of ore. We crisscrossed rugged terrain far removed from towns and highways, accessible only by dirt road or no road at all. When the land became too steep or rugged for a four-wheel drive pickup, we hiked in with pack mules. The mules hauled our gear: tents, sleeping bags, shovels, metal placer pans, canned and freeze-dried food, water jugs, and rifles. I scooped soil into small canvas bags, labeled them by location and soil type (gritty, loamy, clay-like), and loaded the bags onto the mules. The geologists carried compasses, maps, and binoculars with which to orient us in the vast open spaces. It was big country, country to get lost in, scorched in, or find oneself in.

⁓

NEVADA, WESTERN UTAH, and southern Idaho comprise a region known as the Great Basin, a semi-arid region in the western United States encompassing some 206,000 square miles, of which 190,000 are desert. The region is bounded by the Sierra Nevada Mountains on the west, the Wasatch Mountains of Utah on the east, the highlands of the Sonoran desert to the south, and the Columbian Plateau to the north. Its rivers and streams have no outlet to the ocean—they flow into one of many salten lakes, where the water stagnates, evaporates into the air, or sinks into the earth, leaving behind alkalai flats hostile to life. The mountains and highlands once encircled a small ocean teeming with life. Fifteen thousand years ago, a land breach in southern Idaho caused the ocean to drain away through a massive flood with a volume three times the flow of the Amazon River at its mouth. The basin is now dry, silent, and empty, with shrub growth maturing slowly and with difficulty.

Geologists refer to the region as "Basin and Range" due to its inter-mittent series of mountain ranges running north-south, separated by wide valleys covered with sagebrush, cheatgrass, and Russian thistle (tumbleweed). Author and photographer Stephen Trimble calls the basin a "sagebrush ocean," stretching boundlessly across the silent, uninhab-ited spaces. The mountain ranges tower over this sagebrush ocean like enormous islands, just as they once rose out of the watery ocean as real islands.

The region is geologically active. The movement of tectonic plates has stretched the earth's crust throughout much of the basin, creating hot holes, warm ponds, geysers, steam rising through fissures in the earth, and volcanic seepage. The surface appears calm—serene even—but not far under its crust seething, turbulent energies seek to rise through its attenuated skin. Those intense energies have created a molten brew in which heavy metals such as gold and silver get separated out from other minerals.

Geologists at Newmont were certain gold lay hidden in the hills and mountains of northeastern Nevada, even though prospectors discov-ered and removed most of the principal veins of gold and silver ore in the nineteenth and early twentieth centuries. In those earlier times, mining boom towns sprouted throughout Nevada. They had populations of between 500 and 10,000 people, and were home to opera houses, churches, hotels, newspapers, hardware stores, grocers, schools and, of course, saloons and whorehouses. Once the ore gave out, the populations dwindled, turning the once-bustling towns into ghost towns. Only a few decaying buildings and mine tailings—the waste ore dug from the mountainside—remain.

Although miners extracted the principal veins of ore, plenty of gold remains hidden in microscopic flecks diffused over a broad area. Newmont hired my friend Warren and me to help look for it. And we found lots of it, without ever seeing it. Only special assaying can detect it and, until recently, no one knew how to extract it profitably.

Just west of Elko a vein of gold runs northwestward by southeastward through northern Nevada, dipping deep underground at places, rising near the surface in others. The gold is dispersed widely so it is not really accurate to call it a vein; rather, geologists refer to it as a "trend," the "Carlin Trend" to be precise, named after the small town nearby. The trend does not run in a straight line; it twists and turns as it dives and rises. Around 1960, geologists from Newmont Exploration Company discovered where it rises near enough to the surface to extract, and one of the country's most profitable gold mines—the Carlin Gold Mine— sprang to life.

During the summer after my freshman year of college, Warren and I worked at Bootstrap, a site fifteen miles north of the Carlin gold mine, and the home to a small mining operation in the early twentieth century. Prospectors had followed and extracted a vein of gold that ran horizontally through a large hill that stood alone in a great, broad valley. The tunnel, carved through solid rock, remained. Newmont bought the mineral rights and began assessing its gold content.

I did mostly grunt work and heavy lifting, but the pleasure of trekking the backcountry of Nevada made the hard work and scorching daytime heat worthwhile. We worked in shifts around the clock throughout most of the summer. I volunteered for the graveyard shift, from 8:00 P.M. to 5:00 A.M., to avoid the scorching sun with no recourse to shade during the day. At night, the temperature in the high desert dipped to around 50 degrees Fahrenheit—jacket-wearing temperature—contrasted to the mid

90s during the day. Bootstrap was about an hour and a half drive, each way, from Elko, so Newmont provided a small trailer for us to live in during the week. The trailer had no air conditioning, though, so the night crew could not sleep in it during the heat of the day. Instead we slept on cots in the old mining tunnel, where it was cool, dark, and silent. A heavy wooden door at the opening sealed the tunnel enough to keep critters out. Only the howling of distant coyotes broke the silence. Some nights the coyotes came close enough that we could hear their yap-yapping near the door. We were safe within the tunnel, but we kept loaded guns within reach, just in case. The interior of the tunnel presented us with both a temptation to explore and a fear of the unknown. The fear kept us near the opening; none of us ventured into the darkness.

I worked on a drill rig that bored deep into the earth. The rigs used 20-foot steel poles, about five inches in diameter, with a hollow center, to drill down. A steel drill bit was attached to the lower tip of the pole, a bit designed for scouring rock and turning it to dirt. As the drill bore into the ground, an air compressor forced air through the hollow tubes of the poles, blowing the loosened dirt up the shaft to the surface, where I collected it in a tub. I took samples of the soil at five-foot intervals, placed a portion of the dirt in a canvas bag, labeled the bag with a number and, on a separate note pad, noted the depth, color, and consistency of the soil. Once the pole drilled down 20 feet, we attached another to it and continued boring. Each drill rig carried thirty or forty of these poles, so we could drill down 500 to 600 feet if necessary. When the lead bit hit a very hard layer of rock, it wore down, forcing us to raise all the poles out of the ground, one at a time, and replace the steel bit with a diamond one (diamonds are the hardest mineral and can cut through almost anything). Normally we drilled down several hundred feet before moving on to another site fifty yards or so away.

Based on the assay results, geologists created a composite map of the mineral content underground. I marveled at human ingenuity, at the ability to investigate nature, to test, explore, and discover what is beyond the range of our five senses.

I worked with an assistant geologist named Fred Buechel, a gruff, overweight man in his mid-forties. Beuchel had worked for several mining companies before, but had not been promoted to any supervisory role. He was a crank, a heavy drinker, and socially inept. Most of the summer employees disliked his sarcasm and cynicism, but I liked the way he used geological terms as cussword intensifiers, which I suspected he picked up from reading Mark Twain's accounts of Mississippi riverboat pilots. Given his profession, it suited him well. He called prominent land forms by anatomical names (tits, pricks, thumbs, elbows), and sexualized references to digging and drilling into the earth. His language had color. He was once married to a Russian woman he found through an advertisement in the back of some magazine. After receiving her citizenship papers, she divorced him. After that, he despised women. His sole contact with them now was an occasional visit to a whorehouse, which one could find in every town in Nevada. When he went to town for "business," we knew which one.

✧

WARREN AND I HUNTED RATTLESNAKES on occasion (one of the drill rig operators said we could sell their venom for cash because medical researchers used it to produce anti-snake venom). The snakes denned in the cavities of rock outcroppings about 10 miles north of Bootstrap. We took poles made of cut tree branches, about six feet long. The tips, sharpened with our pocket knives, formed a Y-shaped fork that looked like your index and middle finger when you spread them. On our initial hunt, we came across the first rattler on the road to the outcropping. It crossed the road in front of us. We jumped out of the pickup and grabbed our poles. The snake, sensing danger, slithered up the embankment on the side of the road and coiled itself into a small cavity near the top. We poked at it with the tips of our poles, arms stretched—a good-sized rattler can bite through a pair of leather boots, so we kept our distance. The poking made it angry and its rattler buzzed frenetically, but it soon slithered off to escape the annoyance. As it crawled, Warren forked it right behind the head, the pointed tips stuck in the ground. With its head immobilized, the snake couldn't strike. The rest of its body writhed, trying to get free, but it couldn't. Warren grabbed the squirming body with his left hand to hold it still. With his right hand, he firmly grabbed the neck just behind the head as I held the Y-prong tight. I removed the pronged stick so he could lift the snake up. I placed a small glass jar up to the snake's open mouth, its fangs on the inside of the jar and its lower mouth on the outside. The pressure against the fangs forced the snake to secrete its venom into the jar.

We milked five more snakes that day, then let them go. Their venom wouldn't be replenished for some time, so they weren't dangerous. Before driving back to Bootstrap, Warren suggested we take a rattler back for Buechel. I knew just what he had in mind. We caught, milked, and killed another snake and took it back to the tunnel. While Buechel was in town "on business" that evening, we coiled the snake up inside his sleeping bag, then waited up for his return.

As he got into the bag, he recoiled in panic. "Holy crap! There's a fucking snake in there!"

When he heard us snickering, he cursed up some graphic geology words, which grew in number of syllables as he went.

"Goddamn sons of bitches! I'm going to fire your paleozoic asses! Fucking carboniferous potheads!"

In our spare hours, when we weren't hunting snakes, we played cards and drank beer. Beuchel shot at wildlife, mostly lone coyotes and jack rabbits. His rugged temperament seemed just right for these places— places for men in dusty boots who broke rock with handpicks and penetrated the earth with drill rigs and bulldozers. Men who passed the tracks of cougar and deer, and kicked away the shed skin of snakes and bleached antlers, without wonder, seeking no messages, wishing only for a gun. They extracted the gleaming substance of earth, stripped away its mystery, without reverence. I was comfortable among them.

I found solace in the vast, silent spaces, too.

II.

THE MORE TIME I SPENT in the wide-open country, the more I noticed an austere beauty that awakened an inner recess of my psyche that I had not known was there. Like a long, dark mining tunnel, forbidding but also mysterious, I felt lured to explore its depths. Something subtle drew me, though I barely recognized it at first. A sense of the land's awesomeness, even sacredness, filtered gradually into my mind. I had no words to describe it at the time, and even if I had my co-workers, especially Buechel, would have thought me "touched." Treasure of a different kind, I slowly discovered, can be found in out-of-the-way and unexpected places, even this seemingly desolate region.

While contemplating the vastness of the landscape, I began to detect something like a primordial power in nature—could I call it *Spirit*?—that seemed to permeate the countryside. And Spirit is a stealthy hunter. It does not gather in packs to surround you, like coyotes. It does not remain downwind lest you detect its presence. It rides the wind and filters through the grasses, suffusing the quiet, hollow places of the world.

During lunch hour—which for the night shift came around mid-night—we shut down the drill rig for an hour. While the other workers took naps in the pickup trucks, I took solitary walks over the hilltop. I lay on the ground gazing at the stars and listening to the night sounds. I carried a flashlight and a rifle, but on many nights I didn't need the flashlight; moonlight illumined the way. The distant hills and valleys gleamed like quicksilver. Sometimes I thought I sensed a kind of in- and exhalation of the earth, something living, yet invisible. *Is the earth alive? Breathing? Is that possible?* It seemed such a mystery, like when you lean over to hear an infant's soft breath, to detect whether it's still breathing. When you realize it is—what wonder!

One morning, in the tunnel before we fell asleep, Buechel asked, "Where the hell do you go during your lunch breaks? You got a coyote sweetheart out there or something?"

I laughed. "I just wander around. Have you ever really observed the country out there in the moonlight? You can see so far. And it's so quiet. It's eerie, but beautiful."

"Beautiful! This desolate place? There's nothing out there but dust, sagebrush, and coyotes."

"Yeah, but not just those," I protested. "There's beauty, too."

"Yeah, well what's that stuff covering your boots and pant legs every day? And what are those thorns in your socks, *beauty incarnate*?"

I knew just what he meant. The land got so dry it turned powdery. With every step we made, the ground belched a miniature dust cloud that settled on our boots and pant legs. The little burrs from cheatgrass seeds clung to our cotton socks and irritated the skin. We had to stop occasionally to pluck them out.

"But seriously," I said, "there's something mind boggling out there, something mysterious, you know?"

"Oh, Jesus!" he said, "All I see is a bunch of dirt and weeds. Mysterious! You get some sleep so we can go out tomorrow and find more gold. Then you should go invest in Newmont and be rich as hell. They've found a rich lode, for sure. That's why they've brought in more workers—to work the drill rigs around the clock."

"We kind of are already, aren't we?" I said before he finished speaking.

"Kind of what?" he asked.

"Rich. You know, with all that—I don't know." I paused to find the words. "With all that spiritual beauty out there."

Beauty. Spirit. Nature. All kind of mingled and interwoven in ways that were inexplicable to me, as hidden as those flecks of gold, unless you knew how to look for them.

"You're full of it," he said as he turned over on his cot. "The earth's just a lump of inorganic stuff with an itty bitty covering of organic stuff, that's all." I intuited otherwise, but did not have the language with which to express my emerging awareness.

⁓

I BROUGHT MY BIKE TO WORK and began riding in the evenings before my shift began—wandering aimlessly along dirt roads and cow paths. One weekend I didn't return to Elko with the others.

"You're staying here all weekend?" asked Warren. "Alone?"

"Yeah."

He looked at me, puzzled. "What about Jan? Aren't you seeing her this weekend?" Jan and I had dated since high school and usually went out together on weekends. "What's she going to think?"

"If you see her, just tell her I'm working through the weekend."

"Just tell her he's a weirdo!" interrupted Buechel, "that he's got a breccia brain—you take a handful of jagged little rocks and squeeze them together with cement-like mud, and you get a brain like his that doesn't think too keen. If he wants to stay here and commune with dirt, let him."

The next day, I biked on a gravel road leading northward. After half an hour I reached the top of a rise where I caught sight of a vehicle about ten miles away, heading in my direction—not really the *vehicle*, but a cloud of dust billowing upward from a moving point on the road. The dust formed an elongated cloud held aloft by air currents before gradually spreading out and floating back to the ground. I did not want to eat that dust, so I left the road and biked over the untrodden countryside: across creases in the land, through tall sagebrush and Russian thistle that scratched my legs and ankles. I stopped at the edge of a narrow ravine and climbed down it, wondering if I could discern something of its history. Had it formed from the waters of ancient streams, or had the earth cracked and split like wood drying too fast? I rode from one rise to another, horizon to horizon, criss-crossing the valley in a general northward direction, just to see how far the unbounded space could go before I reached something human—a fence, a ranch house, an east-west road, anything. *Such a boundless land.* An inner void, pregnant with something I didn't know, opened as I gazed on the ever-receding horizon. A void at once frightening and comforting. I couldn't explain it.

I came to a large rock outcropping surrounded by brush. One side of the outcropping had a large overhang about six feet up, creating a shady spot—a good place to crawl into and have lunch. I wriggled through the brush on all fours until I got under the ledge and sat with my back against the rock. It was utterly quiet except for a breeze whispering through the brush. A few bird feathers and bones of small animals were scattered here and there. *A hawk must use this place for lunch, too. Good choice.* I wondered if any other human had sat here. Probably not. As I drank water from my canteen, I imagined this recessed nook as a kind of sacred space and thought this: *around the hollow, sacred spaces revolves the busy world that, uneasy with a presence unseen, refuses to know its own quiet center* (or at least some inchoate thought that I later translated into those words). I sat still in the nook, listening. The wind whirled about, raw and pure; it filtered through the brush, gently, rhythmically. The place was lonely; severe; comfortable.

During my walks and bike rides, I began collecting the sheddings and remains of animals: deer antlers, snake skins, golden eagle and hawk feathers, and dry animal bones bleached by the sun. I hung them from the timber just inside the doorway of the tunnel. I hung the jar of snake venom, too (we never bothered to find out where we could sell it). It was my attempt at art. Buechel pretended to scorn my decorations, but I knew he liked them because on one occasion he brought me a badger skull to hang.

"Here's something for your freak art show," he said, and tossed me the skull. A few days later, he brought a coyote tail he'd cut from one of his kills. I hung it with the rest.

One day, Warren and I were assigned a double shift—all night and the next day. We gouged soil samples from the wall of a ten-foot-deep trench dug out by a Caterpillar. After a few hours in the mid-July sun we needed a break. I sat in the last sliver of shade against one wall of the trench. A hard, pointed rock, barely above the surface and hidden by a layer of dirt, jammed into my tail bone. Unwilling to give up the only shady spot around, I began to dig it out. It was firmly lodged. Digging further, I discovered a horn-shaped object extruding from a large boulder below. It was of a different material than the rock, yet encrusted to it. *Could it be the petrified horn of some ancient animal?* It was too thick to be a deer or antelope antler; more like a bull's horn. Yet if buried ten feet underground, it must have been deposited there millennia ago, long before cattle came to this part of the world. Perhaps a buffalo horn? No, it had spiral-like wrinkles around it. It didn't look like any horn I'd seen. I chipped off the extrusion from the rock with a hand pick and stuck it in my ruck sack. In the evening, I showed it to Buechel.

"Do you have any idea what this is?" I asked. He turned it over a couple of times, spat on it, then wiped off the wet dirt with his shirt tail. His facial hair showed several days of growth. He wiped sweat from his forehead with a handkerchief, then examined the object with a magnifying glass.

"Coral" he said. "*Coral rugosa* to be exact."

"Coral? Here? I thought coral grew on the ocean floor, in the tropics."

"It does. Hundreds of millions of years ago, this place used to be under a tropical ocean."

"No way! You're pulling my leg."

"No, I'm not," he said. "The slow movement of tectonic plates shifted the continent way up here. That's a piece of coral, alright, probably from the Devonian period."

"When was that?"

"About 400 million years ago, give or take a few years."

Buechel was a crank, but he knew his geological history.

"So was this thing alive at the same time as the dinosaurs?"

"Earlier. About 150 million years earlier." He paused a while. "If you go over to the Toquima Mountain Range, you'll see plant fossils that are 600 million years old. And I'll tell you something else. Someday the valleys in the Great Basin will be filled with ocean water again. This entire basin is stretching and expanding, just like the Atlantic basin did after North America separated from North Africa. Eventually the stretching will open a breach to the Pacific Ocean— maybe in southern California, maybe in northern California— but when it does, this will be ocean again, and a big chunk of California will be an island. The Humboldt River and all the smaller streams will have an outlet to the ocean instead of emptying into alkalai flats. That's inevitable. Probably not before we get the gold out of this hill, though." Beuchel, it seemed, knew something about the geological future, too. *How could someone who knew the deep history of this land not see beauty in it?*

I held the coral up to have a close look. "So this thing lived 400 million years ago?"

"Yeah. Maybe only 398 million."

"Ah, so it's not very old, then."

"Nah. Not much older than your mama," he said.

"Your mama, maybe," I said as I tied a string around a wrinkle of the coral and hung it along with the coyote tail, deer antlers, and other items. I pondered my decorations.

"Could any of these animals hanging here have descended from this coral? You know, maybe the coral evolved into an animal and one of these things is its descendent," I said.

"Probably not, but you might be, with that fucking precambrian fossil brain of yours."

III.

IT WAS THE NIGHT OF the full red moon of August. We had finished our work at Bootstrap several weeks earlier. We knew it was time to move on when the big yellow earth movers started arriving. Mining engineers, geologists, and surveyors wandered the hillside, surveying, calculating, pointing things out to one another on maps and drawings. Newmont would soon blast the hill with dynamite and shovel loads of earth into the giant trucks, which would haul the ore to the Carlin Gold mine for crushing and heap-leaching.

In a typical heap-leach operation, miners remove tons of ore from hillsides or open pits, crush it into dirt, and pile it onto clay or plastic liners. They then spray large quantities of cyanide solution over the ore. As the cyanide percolates through the layers of dirt, it draws microscopic flecks of gold and extracts up to ninety-seven percent of it from the rest of the ore. This "pregnant" solution concentrates at the bottom of a drainage system, where the miners distill and process it further. We completed our work without seeing a speck of gold. Buechel had predicted it right; the increased activity and earth movers confirmed it.

Newmont sent Buechel and me to the Prospect Mountains in central Nevada, just south of Eureka—a nineteenth-century boom town now turned into a lethargic community of around 350 inhabitants. As we drove through town, we noticed a handful of old-timers sitting on benches in front of decaying buildings.

"What do you think these old guys do all day long?" I asked.

"They probably reminisce about the old days and hope a new deposit of gold gets discovered so the town can spring back to life with saloons and whorehouses."

Buechel and I explored the region surrounding Prospect Peak, the highest mountain in the range at 10,400 feet, and the site of significant mining operations in the 19th century. Extensive tailings fanned out from the mouth of several tunnels. Tons of dirt had been removed, so the tunnels went in deep, perhaps forming honey-combs inside the mountain. We planned to spend two weeks there.

I collected soil samples at 100-foot intervals while Buechel analyzed rock outcroppings and applied drops of chemicals to the dirt I dug up. He smelled and licked chips of rock he broke off with his hand pick, tasting for hints of certain minerals. We worked our way gradually over a nine-square-mile area, with frequent stops, side trips around ravines, and slow climbs up the mountainside. Because of Buechel's weight, he had to take it slow. We pitched a tent alongside a spring and in the evenings gathered firewood and cooked our meals. We hunted cottontail or grouse for dinner.

The alpine terrain, well above the sagebrush zone, boasted rich grasses, berries, pinyon pine, wildflowers, and springs—good country for sheep-grazing. We chanced upon a flock almost daily. A Basque sheepherder made a point of visiting us regularly, glad for human contact. He spent nights alone in a metal-covered wagon stationed near the bottom of the canyon. He rode up the mountain on horseback each day to check on the flocks and share wine with us from a leather bota. He spoke little English, so we conversed in pidgin and by gesture.

One morning Beuchel and I discovered two dead sheep lying in the brush. We walked over to have a closer look. As we approached we saw others. Three. Four. Five. Then many others, twenty-three in all. Dead sheep strewn everywhere.

"What the hell happened here?" I asked.

"Dunno," said Buechel. "Maybe they ate some poisonous plants clustered in the area."

Later that day, we met the sheepherder and pointed out the site to him. On the following day, rangers from the Fish and Wildlife Service came to inspect the scene. They determined a lone mountain lion had killed them, not for food, but for sport. None of the sheep—not one— had been eaten.

Buechel and I did not sleep in the tent that night or out in the open, knowing a killer was on the loose. We slept in one of the mining tunnels on the side of Prospect Peak. Its shabby wooden door closed well enough. We kept our loaded rifles nearby.

The night witch set loose by the full moon forbade me sleep. I lay for a long time on the cot, pondering the great expanse of geological time and our miniscule span of life within it. Though just a microscopic fleck within its enormity, I felt a strange kindredness toward it. I wanted to walk about, but dared not because of the cougar. I decided to explore the tunnel instead. I put on my boots, grabbed a flashlight and rifle, and walked into the darkness.

I shone light on the walls and felt the layers of earth, one upon another. How old are these rocks, I wondered? If an ancient coral fossil ten or twelve feet below the surface was 400 million years old, how old was this rock deep inside the mountain? A billion? It boggled the mind.

The tunnel went straight into the mountain for at least a hundred yards, then branched off in three directions. I took the branch on the right, the wider one. After another hundred feet or so, the tunnel descended steadily, deeper into the darkness. More branches. Then cross branches. Again I took the larger one, reasoning it would be the main branch. By following the larger tunnel consistently, I should be able to find my way back. After a time, the air became tight. It grew warmer. Another branch veered to the left. I began following a rise. The vein of ore must have trended horizontally, then twisted downward before gradually ascending. Walking became labored, breathing more difficult, though I was used to climbing hills. I stopped frequently to catch my breath. *Altitude sickness?* I felt a momentary disorientation. What if I got lost in this maze of passageways? Would Buechel think to look for me here? He was accustomed to my nighttime walks; he would assume I had gone outside; would look for me in the morning, and wonder if the mountain lion had dragged me off to its lair.

What would happen if I died in here? Would they find me? If not, I imagined two endings. One was this: if Newmont found gold, they would tear down this mountain, and my remains would end up in a heap-leach pile, dissolved by cyanide. The second was less dispiriting. The earth's movement would close the tunnel and fuse my bones with Devonian or Ordovician rock. Some geologist would discover them ten million years from now and place them on exhibit as an example of a primitive hominoid form. Viewers would speculate on what thoughts I might have had and what dreams and promises I never fulfilled. Would they be able to deduce from DNA that I *had* thoughts and dreams? Could scientists, by then, *recreate* my memories—such as bike rides toward a boundless horizon? Could they recreate the wonder and mystery of that?

I continued along the passageway. If I got lost, I could shout for help from Buechel—if he could hear me, anyway. I imagined him banging on a placer pan repetitively, and I would follow the sound back. That image led to a curious question, given the circumstances: Would I even want to shout for help from Beuchel? Would death be any worse than the smirk on his face when I found my way back? I could hear his words, "Hey,

Tonto, did you find some creature back there with an Archaean brain like yours?" Yet, I knew he would worry.

Soon I noticed a musty, acrid smell. And foul. Was it the *odor of death?* It grew stronger. Soon I entered a widened chamber, a small cavern of sorts. I shone light all around. There were bat droppings agglomerated on one side wall. They spread onto the floor, rank and hot, the outer layer still moist. Ghoulish stuff. I started to turn back, but then noticed there were no bats. They must be outside, hunting insects. There had to be an opening somewhere nearby. How else could they get out? I continued past the chamber. Soon a hint of outside air mingled with the musty, stale air of the tunnel. As the outside air became stronger, I perceived a soft light up ahead. It came from an opening above, right where the tunnel came to an end.

A wooden ladder, old and decrepit, rose to the opening. Why did the miners use this opening? They couldn't have hauled ore out through here. An escape route, probably. Two of the ladder's rungs were missing, others were creaky. I pressed against it, shook it, pulled on the rungs within reach, stood on the bottom one. It was usable. I carefully ascended.

Outside, the full moon glowed fiery orange, not far above the eastern horizon. I walked to the top of Prospect Peak to get the best view and peered over what seemed the edge of the world. To the north, a few dim lights from Eureka shone in the distance. In all directions, the sky extended limitlessly, and the earth seemed to stretch out with it. The great valley below waited expectantly, like a womb, to be filled with glory. There was a mountain range thirty miles beyond, and another, ninety miles, stretching like millenia over the vast empty spaces. The moon's light bathed the earth in a soft sheen like the lustre of the ocean just after sunset, or before sunrise. *Yes, yes, Spirit hovers over these boundless spaces. Seeps in and fills them. The great valleys are like lungs through which it breathes in and out, rhythmically, glacially.* The moonlight was gold, space infinite, and Spirit rested patiently, everywhere. I knew this, though I was unschooled in things spiritual. Something broad and expansive filled me. And I intuited this, too: the long decades and distances between saints are too much. We no longer expect to hear, out of those silent spaces, a word that will bless. ❧

2016 Finalist

Kimberly Meyer

PROJECT DESCRIPTION

"Sewage Pilgrimage" is an account of my journey as I retraced the pilgrimage of a Dominican priest, Felix Fabri, who had traveled to the Holy Land and Mount Sinai in 1483. For almost two months, I followed the priest's path, eventually crossing from Israel into the wilderness of the Sinai Desert. I discovered that 12 million gallons of raw sewage a day pour out of Jerusalem into the Kidron River that traverses both Israel and the Palestinian Territories, making this cultural and spiritual treasure a wasteland, held hostage to the political impasse between its leaders.

The desert is the spiritual heart of Judaism, Christianity, and Islam, says Avner Goren, a leading Israeli archaeologist, who oversaw operations in the Sinai Desert during the years that Israel controlled the peninsula. Goren, who I met in Israel last summer after my journey to Sinai (and who serves as guide to Bruce Feiler in *Walking the Bible*), has a vision for the Kidron Valley of the Judean Desert: a pilgrimage trail that would thread outward from the Old City all the way to the salt sea that separates Israel from Jordan, interrupted only by shelters manned by local Bedouin, desert nomads who could offer traditional hospitality.

Because of that impasse, cultural sites have gone neglected, endemic species are disappearing, groundwater sources are threatened, and much of the fertile farmland along the river has been abandoned. But Goren and others—Israeli lawyers and architects and planners, the Greek Orthodox monks of Mar Saba monastery, and Palestinian educators and entrepreneurs—are working subversively beyond official channels to stop this desecration. If they succeed, and clean the river and lay down the pilgrimage path beside the river that is now filled with trash, they will both literally and figuratively connect Palestinians and Israelis. The route through this contested landscape will become a bridge.

What the Desert Said

AT THE BEGINNING OF THE THIRD BOOK of the *Odyssey*,
Telemachus' ship pulls into the harbor of sandy Pylos, as the morning
light burnishes the sea. Homer tells us how

> *The sun rose from the still, beautiful water*
> *Into the bronze sky, to shine upon the gods*
> *And upon men who die on the life-giving earth.*

Though that sun dawns upon gods and men alike, this is how we
humans are defined: as the men who die. We are not the gods, the *athan-
atoi*, as the original Greek has it—the ones *without death*, and therefore
beyond time. Instead, we are bound by time. We may once have walked
in a garden with the Lord of all creation, but we've been banished to a
land of thorn and thistle, and the life-giving earth from which we were
made now folds us back into its dust at the end of our days. The time of
timelessness is over.

And yet the ache for that state of timelessness remains. We seek it in
sacred places, which mark off a space from the ravages of the time-bound
world that our mortal bodies inhabit. When Yahweh calls out to Moses
from the midst of the bush that burned with fire but was not consumed,
he is marking off sacred space—the place where He will appoint Moses
to lead the Israelites out of Egypt and to their homeland of Canaan.
"Draw not nigh hither, "Yahweh commands, "put off thy shoes from off
they feet, for the place whereon thou standest is holy ground." So holy
that *seneh*, the Hebrew word for "bush," perhaps even gave the Sinai its
name. When, centuries later, the Roman Empress Helena ordered that a
Chapel of the Burning Bush be built at the base of Mount Sinai to commemorate this moment, she too was marking off sacred space. And when
the miracle is remembered by pilgrims who travel to the desert to put off

their shoes and stand inside that church, it is still happening, it is always happening, and time, and our subjection to it, is therefore, annulled.

Last summer, my daughter, Ellie, and I attempted to retrace the path of one such pilgrim, a Dominican priest from Ulm, Germany, who had traveled to the Holy Land and Mount Sinai in 1483. This friar, Felix Fabri, had written an account of his journey, one filled with tangible details— traversing the dry Judean hills by donkey, paying tolls to the Saracen lords of Jerusalem, kissing the bodily relics of saints—of travel in the Age of Faith. I'd stumbled across his *Book of Wanderings* in the library years before and been inexplicably transfixed. My preoccupation seemed in some ways especially mystifying given the precarious state of my immortal soul, which had been in self-imposed exile from the Kingdom of God for the better part of my life. All that time, I stood on the outside of faith, my face peering in through the bars of the gates of the garden, while the cherubim with their whirling swords of flame kept me at bay. But in my exile, I was haunted. By God, maybe. Or maybe by a longing for evidence to refute my fear that this material world is all there is. Perhaps God and this longing are one. It's not that I thought I would find either God or solace for my fears by retracing Fabri's path. I knew that he traveled through a world still enchanted by belief, a world that for me was irrevocably shorn of magic and miracles. And yet I went.

A restlessness seemed to drive Fabri. "I call God to witness that for many years I was in such a fever of longing to perform that pilgrimage that whether I was asleep or awake I hardly ever had any other subject before my mind," Fabri writes. "And I may say with truth that while engaged in these thoughts I lay awake for more than a thousand hours of the night and time of rest." A similar restlessness had driven me. For almost two months, my daughter and I followed Fabri from Ulm to Venice, where he had boarded a pilgrim galley. We followed him as he sailed along the Dalmatian Coast and through Greece and Cyprus. We followed him through the port of Jaffa into Jerusalem, and then across the Negev. Here, on this very spot, we were told at all the churches and monasteries and historical monuments we visited, here, right here, touch it, bless your rosary upon it, a miracle occurred. Maybe a martyrdom. Maybe a sermon. Maybe a last supper. Maybe a birth or death or resurrection. By the time we reached Taba, where we crossed from Israel into the wilderness of the Sinai Desert on our way to St. Catherine's Monastery and the Chapel of the Burning Bush, our capacity for wonder was severely frayed.

For days, we navigated the *wadis*, dry riverbeds running through the desert, in the jeep of Sheik Swelam, a sinewy chain-smoking Bedouin in *jalabiya* and *keffiyeh* and Ray-Bans, who brought with him his sullen twelve-year-old son, and Mohammad, an Egyptian interpreter, fresh from the Revolution in Tahrir Square. As we drove across the bottom of what was once an ancient ocean, we stared out of the open windows at pale sandstone formations, some crouched on the desert floor like sphinxes, some like fallen temples. The red stone hills in the distance seemed chiseled and carved like a frieze. Others were round as if turned on a potter's wheel. But the sphinxes, the temples, the friezes are just similes: *like* or *as*. In reality, there were no monuments here trying to stay the passage of time. No monuments marking anything at all. And in this vast desert, we seemed to be the only breathing, moving things. Everywhere, the relentless sun was shining upon men who die on the life-giving earth.

⁜

AS FELIX FABRI AND HIS PILGRIM BAND, led by an Arab guide, leave Gaza and that last outpost of civilization recedes behind them, the pitilessness of the terrain, their own relentless thirst, the breadth of the endless waste take hold. "In these plains we saw neither men nor beasts, neither villages, houses, trees, grass, nor bushes, but only the sandy earth, parched by the sun's heat," he writes on the 11th of September, 1483. In the afternoon, they enter a land of swelling hills. In the valley between them, the travelers pitch their tents. The camel drivers head off with jars and water-skins to fetch fresh water from a cistern, while the pilgrims spread out in search of firewood. They find only dry bushes—*seneh*—which they pull up by the roots.

"This place was called in Arabic *Chawatha*, and here we found many proofs that once human dwellings had stood there," Fabri writes, "for we found above us twelve great ancient walled cisterns, round about which lay many broken bricks, broken pots, and ashes from smiths' forges... In the cisterns we saw the dead bodies of great and terrible serpents, and of animals unknown to us." On the morning of the 12th, they load the camels early, before daylight, and depart from *Chawatha* together in the dark.

❧

ALTHOUGH THE DAYS OF CAMEL CARAVANS, like the days of miracles, are over, I had insisted on riding camels in the desert. So Sheik Swelam hired camels for us that first afternoon. Often we paused to let the camels graze on clumps of spiny grasses, their heads on their necks moving periscopically, their gaze, like their chewing, ruminative. We passed through an abandoned Bedouin camp, detritus of detritus: nylon fencing, wood scraps, oil drums, empty and tattered rice bags. Later we saw acacia trees tied with bits of fading fabric, precarious stacks of flat stones. "Signs," said Mohammad, though of what he did not say. Of the presence of humans? The way through the desert? Portents of the divine? We tried to read the engravings on the desert walls—camels and goats scratched into the sandstone surface, strange rows of vertical lines. What did they mean? There were fragments of Arabic, nearly worn away— *Bismillahir Rahmanir Rahim, In the name of Allah, the Most Beneficent, the most Merciful.*

We came across a wizened elderly sheik and his plump younger wife in the shadow of a rock formation, the shade like the curve of the lunula of a fingernail. They sat on a rug beside their jeep. When we pulled up, the woman covered her head. Over a small fire, she made us sweet tea in a tin vegetable can rinsed clean, then poured the tea into two small, clear glasses. Later, when the glasses were rinsed and refilled for Sheik Swelam and Mohammad, and again for the sullen son, I realized that these were the only ones they had. While Sheik Swelam and the couple talked, Ellie and I looked out together on the endless floor of the former sea, lined by bisque-colored buttes and mesas, sky and sky and sky. Mohammad said the couple were speaking together with Sheik Swelam in an older Arabic, one brought by their ancestors when these desert nomads came, like Abraham, with their camels and goats and their wool tents and woven rugs from Arabia centuries ago. In some unfathomable way, that ancient tongue they spoke seemed connected to the faded etchings on the walls of the canyons.

❖

IN THE DESERT, TIME SLOWED AND stretched, or maybe condensed, thickening like a reduction in which all excess is boiled away. Or perhaps that is only how it was in my mind, or now, in my memory of it. In the mornings, Sheik Swelam, a cigarette dangling from his lips, makes milky Nescafe over a fire of a few twigs, washing out the clear glasses with a swill of water, elegantly whirling and rubbing with his thumb at the same time. We sit on the rugs from the jeep in silence, eating flatbread and soft white cheese and jam. Then all day we drive the *wadis,* stopping at a Bedouin camp where we all drink tea and Sheik Swelam and Mohammad smoke cigarettes with men possessed of piercing eyes and stained teeth. Later, in the shade of an acacia tree or a sandstone cliff, lunch and a rest. Then we drive on. From time to time, Sheik Swelam veers off the *wadi* to a well he remembers, and he fills the water jugs, protected by cloth covers embroidered by the women—distant figures against the hills in black shawls and long black robes, young children on their hips, surrounded by shaggy goats. At the wells, Ellie and I bend over while Sheik Swelam pours the cold water down our necks, wetting our hair, keeping us cool in the intense desert heat, heat like a kiln, heat without relief. Later in the afternoon, when he spots a band of shrubs in the parched riverbeds, we get out of the jeep and, like the medieval pilgrims, we gather dried branches of the desert bushes to burn. Towards evening, in a gully or in an encampment or at an oasis, Mohammad and the sheik and his wordless son pull out the sleeping bags and the food and the pots and plates, and while Ellie and I try to find a hidden place to wash the desert sand out of the pores of our faces, they cook for us— chicken and vegetables, flatbread, a thick fava bean stew. We fall asleep beneath the stars as the fire dies down. No voice calls out to us from the midst of the burning.

❖

FOR FABRI AND THE MEDIEVAL PILGRIMS who make their punishing journey that late summer and early fall of 1483, the desert wilderness of the Sinai is sacred, the Word of God made Flesh. Although their bodies are at the mercy of this brutal place on the map, they cross a spiritual landscape that exists beyond time, beyond the physical world that makes their bodies suffer. As he travels, Fabri thinks about the symbolic nature of the desert. It is, he says, a wasteland, abandoned by God, "as though [He] had used it to improve or adorn the rest of the universe. The country," he goes on, "seems also forsaken by the heavens, for it lacks the kindly influence of the stars, and seems to be viewed angrily by them, and, as it were, turned into iron, while the heaven above seems harsh, pitiless, and brazen." Because of this harshness, he says, the desert has always been a site of testing and temptation. But it is also where God bestowed the commandments upon his wandering people. It's where manna rained down, and water burst forth from stone. It's a place of retreat from the world, and of devotion and contemplation. You can be found here. At the same time, you can easily get lost, for through the desert there is no fixed path.

❧

I NEVER KNEW WHERE I was in the desert. Not only were we untethered from time, we were untethered from space as well. As we passed from *wadi* to *wadi*, I wrote down their names in my notebook: *Wadi Razala, Wadi Lathi, Wadi Watir.* But without a map to pin them to, the names meant nothing.

Lunch one day beneath a gnarled acacia tree, the only shade to be found. Tomatoes and cucumbers, canned tuna with chopped onions, white cheese, tea, unleavened bread. The only sounds: flies, the wind. Ellie and I lie on mats beneath the delicate leaves of the acacia and read. The son sleeps in the jeep. I ask the sheik where, exactly, we are. With a stick, he draws a map in the dirt of where we've been, one *wadi* branching off into another like a bare tree in winter. Looking out across the expanse of sand and scrub, he tells me he could travel this land day or night. "Everything I have in here," he says, tapping his head.

That night we camped in a ravine, at the point where two *wadis* meet, one flowing to the Gulf of Suez, the other to the Gulf of Aqaba, a tipping point, a hinge of the earth. During dinner, cooked over the small fire pit fueled by splinters of *seneh* we'd collected that afternoon, Sheik Swelam had pointed off to the Milky Way far south of us and said that when it's centered over the southern sky, then the fruit of the date palms is most sweet. After the dishes had been washed, and the others had closed their eyes, I lay in the dark looking up at the sky feeling microscopic, mitochondrial in the vastness.

I said no voice called out to us from the midst of the burning fire. But sometime in the night, I woke up in the darkness, shivering in the dry desert air. The fire had turned to cold ash, and the whole world had stilled, as if it was holding its breath, waiting for a revelation. Maybe it was only the chill that sharpened my mind, or maybe it was the divine nudging me awake so that I might see, but I opened my eyes that night to the clarity of the stars, so near my face and bright that it seemed a universe of light was trying to press itself through the curved veil of dark sky above me. I was not so much looking *at* things as looking *through* them to something beyond. The turning earth had carried the Milky Way straight above us by this motionless hour, and, for a moment, I saw the sky as a topographical map of another world, the white, ridged cloud of the Milky Way like a chain of mountains, and the countless stars like the towns and villages and cities of a country I didn't know. I imagined that other world, gazing out at us, the desert I inhabited its firmament, any living creature there looking up in wonder at us lying in these heavens of sand. How much is hidden, I thought, by the deceptive light of day. How little we actually see of what exists.

But in the cold illumination of the morning, as Sheik Swelam washed his face and lit a fire, it seemed again that the days of revelation might be over. That there are only, if we are lucky, small moments of clarity that open something in us amid the clamor and confusion. And then the void closes up like a wound, the ache only vaguely remembered.

❖

"EVERYTHING I HAVE IN HERE," Sheik Swelam had said, like one of the ancient bards who sang from memory of gods and heroes and men who die on the life-giving earth. How lightly the Bedouin travel, how little they carry, how few marks they make. Everywhere on this trip, Ellie and I had seen monuments built by human hands to commemorate and mark and remember. Even Fabri's account was a shrine of memory, his experiences encased in words. "I never passed one single day while I was on my travels," he wrote to his Dominican brethren, "without writing some notes, not even when I was at sea, in storms, or in the Holy Land; and in the desert I have frequently written as I sat on an ass or a camel; or at night, while the others were asleep, I would sit and put into writing what I had seen."

I wanted to write it all down too—sweet tea made in a tin can and the curve of shade at the base of the curve of a mesa, a Bedouin woman, glint of black against the dun-colored sand, a sky punctured by stars. This attempt to pluck ephemera from the flux of experience and to pin them in words is also, like the building of monuments, the marking out of sacred space. It encloses the past, removes it from time, and tries to keep it alive in its own private Eden. But of course this is impossible—to capture any moment and take it home as a souvenir.

One morning, Fabri and his pilgrim band enter the region of *Wadi el-Arish*. On their right rise mountains of exceeding whiteness; on their left, an expanse of black stone and sand, "scorched as though a fire had lately burned everything that would burn therein." Fabri asks his guide where this wilderness ends, and the guide replies that no living man has ever been to the end of it. Because for Fabri this desert wilderness is sacred territory, because it is both spiritual and actual, he imagines that abutting the boundary of these plains must be the earthly paradise where time stands still, "and therefore the flashings of the fiery sword, which the Lord has placed before the entrance to paradise, has scorched these plains and forbids all approach." But paradise is manifestly there.

In the Sinai Peninsula that my daughter and I crossed, the only monument is the desert itself, and what's remembered is only in the mind. A few marks on the rock walls, a few stacks of stones, bright rags tied in trees. The Bedouin who inhabit this precarious land seem to recognize of necessity how flimsy are the things made, how soon they will pass away. And this recognition is, it seemed to me as we drove over the impenetrable surface of it, a humble submission to this essential fact of human existence: our fragility in this transitory world. We are the men who die on the life-giving earth.

After every meal, Sheik Swelam would scrape the plastic plates clean, and wash them with water from the jugs we carried in the jeep, then throw what couldn't be saved into the fire. The scrapings he would leave on a flat stone for the desert animals.

This is what the desert said: Carry only what you need. Burn what can't be saved. Leave the remnants as an offering. ⌇

(Originally published in *Ploughshares,* Fall 2012.)
(Kimberly Meyer's book, *The Book of Wanderings: A Mother-Daughter Pilgrimage,* was published by Little, Brown and Company.)

2015 Winner

Rebecca Lawton

PROJECT DESCRIPTION

The Oasis this Time is a work of creative nonfiction about California fan palm oases, barometers of the effects of falling groundwater in communities around the American West. I will return to the U.C. Irvine Steele-Burnand Research Station in the Anza Borrego Desert, California. The landscape and the community will be my research foci.

I will meet with community members, scientists, developers, agricultural people, visitors, and other writers/artists to explore how water is viewed in the Anza Borrego valley. I will also visit palm oases to make detailed observations of flora and fauna (my metaphorical gold) within the oasis zones and their surroundings. The U.C.I. Reserve Manager, Jim Dice, and the visiting researchers (many of whom study water issues) will help provide valuable access to field locations and experts.

My initial research in early 2015 informed me that some claim Borrego Springs has 500 years of capacity left in the groundwater (its current water supply). Others who have studied the aquifer and its recharge potential say there are no more than twenty years of supply available at today's use. Most of the groundwater is pumped for agriculture (70%); the second highest use is for irrigation of golf courses and to water the spas (20%). The town and wild ecosystems receive the remaining 10%.

What I love about the study location is its open, quirky town, dyed-in-the-wool desert people, and wildlife: the 10 percenters. The California fan palm is an icon for this group: as goes groundwater, so goes the *Washingtonia*-fringed oasis. My project will be an enduring piece of desert literature on the oasis in the context of a society that still irrigates fairways and grapefruit with 10,000-year-old groundwater.

Water-intensive uses exhaust the aquifer and imperil the future of communities and ecosystems. By helping advance the palm oases of Borrego into song and story, I will advance awareness of the critical water supply that sustains them and us, a critical piece of desert literacy.

The Sentinels

THE TOWN OF TWENTYNINE PALMS, CALIFORNIA, is as
hushed as a morgue. Chairs sit empty in barbershops advertising marine
haircuts for ten bucks. There are no families in the shops and cafés, no
moms holding kids by the hand—just a quiet, Mojave Desert main street
with traffic passing through. In a wind that hasn't given up its spring
chill, yellow ribbons stream from lightpoles, street signs, storefronts.
They're a faithful promise to endure, based on a pop song once played to
death on the radio. The faded ribbons, bleached white on folds and curls,
say that the waiting has gone on too long. Among stubby stands of sage
and creosote, houses stand with drapes drawn to the ever-present sun.
Inside, the residents must still be holding vigil, believing in the inevitable
return of the warrior.

Lured by the call of anything wet, I check into the first motel I see. I
find my air-conditioned room, pull on my bathing suit, wrap up in a big
white towel, and wander out the back door in search of a hot tub.

A young marine greets me from a bistro table beside the water. He's
a junior officer, probably just a few years older than my own teenaged
daughter. His face reveals no guile, especially when he smiles. He tells me
he's been assigned to an advanced course in communications.

He also volunteers an answer to the unasked question. "The base is
dead quiet because everyone's overseas." He's stuck in town while others
in his unit have been sent to Iraq.

Although the water is lovely and inviting, he has his back to it—he's
in uniform, with a textbook spread before him. When he's done with his
course, he'll ship out, too. The reading doesn't bother him, except that
it requires "too much math." He says it in all earnestness, with no irony
about the key role of numbers in his job. To him, they pose just one more
barrier to getting to fight.

When I tell him I'm visiting from the northern part of the state, he asks if I've heard about a tank crew lost near Nasiriyah, Iraq. After some back and forth, I realize that I have: the gunner, a Scottish-born newly-wed, lives close to my longtime hometown near San Francisco. The local paper has run a series on his going missing. His wife is expecting their first child any day.

"It's an M1A1 Abrams crew," he tells me. "They're based here, in Twentynine Palms."

I ask if he has updates. He does. The remaining members of the First Tank Battalion have no clue to the missing crew's whereabouts. The last radio contact from the Abrams came in before midnight Tuesday, when the tank was patrolling without headlights west of the Euphrates River. Today is Thursday. Desert sandstorms and near-zero visibility have made search efforts impossible. Blowing sand has confined the rest of the battalion to their quarters. Photographs in the paper show the men praying together in a dimly lit building.

"Doesn't it scare you?" I ask. "That an entire tank and its crew can disappear like that?"

The officer shakes his head. "Going MIA is one risk you take. And casualties are part of combat."

My heart beats so hard I wonder if he can hear it. Probably not. He goes back to his books with the calm of a Zen priest.

Should I pray? Make a wish? Some months ago a friend taught me a time-tested method for wishing: fix your gaze on the nearest natural object and compose an eight-syllable blessing. My eyes go to a row of palm trees in the motel garden. I count out syllables on both hands. *Please. Find the crew. Alive and well.*

I unwrap from my towel and settle into the hot tub. Occasionally I check on the officer out of the corner of my eye. Now he's pressing buttons on his calculator, writing on a notepad, flipping through the textbook. He's eager, clearly, but how can he be so calm? As a Colorado River guide in the 1970s, I spent years working among veterans just home from fighting in Southeast Asia: former US Navy Seals, US Army Special Forces, US Marine Corps Enlisted—they could no more consider shipping out again than they could walk on water.

The hot-tub jets time out. The officer lifts his head. "Don't get up. I'll take care of it." He speaks with dignity, as if bearing a torch of responsibility for his mother or a favorite aunt.

I let him handle it for me.

I'VE COME TO THE DESERT for the waters: specifically oases. My heart has been captured by spring-fed groves of California fan palm since I was in grade school. Whispering *Washingtonia filifera,* hiding in canyons. Their secretive ways. During most spring breaks, although we lived two states away, our parents drove south from our home outside Portland, Oregon, through the days and into the nights, with four little kids in the backseat. South from the Columbia River, down the Willamette Valley, with snow-draped Cascade Mountains to the east. South through the Central Valley with the Sierra Nevada rising up from greening foothills. We skirted Los Angeles as best we could. Mostly we kids read comic books while our parents did all the work, found some campsite or motel with space every night, and made sure we were fed, clean, and not bickering. Destination: Palm Canyon Campground, Anza-Borrego Desert State Park east of San Diego, an arid haven of picnic tables under palm-frond *palapas* and windbreaks constructed of rock dug from nearby alluvial fans.

Most days we hiked up Palm Canyon or some other trail into the desert hills. The paths wound past white blossomed agave, red fans of blooms on the ocotillos, waxy petals of flowers on the prickly pear cactus. We paused in awe when we caught a glimpse of a coyote's tail as it fled or picked out herds of desert bighorn sheep from cliffs they matched exactly. We endured the bird obsession of our mother, the times she stopped without warning to scan an inauspicious shrub with binoculars. She did manage eventually to make passionate birders of her husband and a few of her children; at the time, though, we small ones had little patience for standing statue still to glimpse a nesting oriole or cactus wren.

Back then in Palm Canyon, most of the trees had long, full frond skirts, untouched by fire. Subsequently the trees were set ablaze by "careless" hikers, according to today's state park signs. Back then, though, the rustle of palm fronds set the soundscape. No traffic noise. Few human voices. A clear-running stream fell over boulders, pooled in little basins, ran free over pebbles and gravel. Here there were no school tests, no student cliques, no yearning for recess. Who even had thoughts of going home? The oasis became a cherished refuge, a place where every molecule of water in our bodies could rest among peaceful canopies of *Washingtonia*.

At the entrance to Joshua Tree National Park, 130 miles northeast of our beloved Anza Borrego and one mile from downtown Twentynine Palms, stands a tiny palm oasis of the same numerical name. A fertility legend attached to it endures, repeated in newspapers, motel advertisements, and desert-rat tour books. It's a mythical place not to be missed, the accounts say. The oasis is the town's forebear, a stopover for travelers since prehistoric times. On my second morning in the area, I cross the motel lobby on my way out to find the storied refuge. Through gleaming windows, I spot the officer at work again by the pool and think immediately of the missing tank crew. Headlines in the motel's newspaper rack tell me nothing. Hoping for good news later, I duck out to conduct my search: a short drive, a nearly empty parking lot at the National Park Service visitor center, a paved path to well tended stands of *Washingtonia*.

In movies filmed in the desert, desperate, thirst crazed pilgrims plunge into oases head first. The ubiquitous presence of water belies the fact that an oasis may not be wet at all. The hydric zone may be a spring or pool, true, but it is just as likely to be wet earth indicating groundwater near the surface. Here there is neither pool nor dampness. There's no open pool anywhere, no yearned-for expanse of blue. Not only that, the surrounding oasis proper isn't the obvious circle of palms, the stuff of kneeling camels and silk swathed sheikhs. Instead, just a few palms string along the trails here—hardly a circle, at least not at first glance. The third and outer zone, the desert-oasis ecotone, is sparse. It's not so different from the surrounding desert that lurks like a cruel bar bouncer on the outside of the precious palms.

Later I'll read that the marshy, ecologically diverse center of the Twentynine Palms oasis dried up some thirty years ago. Declines in groundwater desiccated the springs watering vegetation and wildlife. Monitoring of groundwater wells by the California Department of Water Resources has shown the impact of a training base, a town, and the visitation of over 140,000 souls annually. Between 1939 and 2013, water levels dropped seventy feet and more beneath Twentynine Palms.

Even without open water, the little shade of the oasis beckons. Visitors are fenced out, though, because the weight of our trespass would damage the trees' root systems. *Washingtonia* has pencillate rootlets just inches underground that reach as far as twenty feet from the trunk. Their job is to search for shallow groundwater. Too many pedestrians, no matter how appreciative our hearts, would trample and compress the soil supporting the vulnerable network. The palms are therefore barred with handrails and threats of hefty fines. We spectators stick to the trails and hold onto our cash.

Even with the park's best efforts, the trees at Twentynine Palms fail to send their shallow roots to moisture. The water table has simply dropped too far. To keep the oasis alive, National Park Service staff regularly apply water directly to the base of the palms. They irrigate.

Interpretive signs further the fertility legend, as well as a second name for the oasis: *Mara* or *Marah*, meaning "big springs and much grass." The word derives from Native American lexis—probably the Serrano language. In the legend, indigenous women of the Mojave traveled to the oasis specifically to give birth to sons. Archaeological studies may not support that, but they do document habitation by Native Americans in the area, first Serrano and Cahuilla then Chemehuevi, millennia before it became a base for men about to wage war. Footpaths radiate out from the once abundantly marshy Mara, a hub of prehistoric comings and goings. A count of 480 bone fragments in excavations at the site evidence a prehistoric human diet of largely black tailed jackrabbit and desert tortoise, as well as lesser amounts of desert bighorn sheep, mule deer, smaller mammals, birds, and reptiles. For a time, a settlement near Mara served as home or camp for those foraging the nearby alluvial fans and hills.

The total number of palms at Mara, however, has not been recorded as twenty-nine; rather, oral and written accounts beginning in the 1800s note fewer than twenty. Even at the time of European contact, palms numbered in the teens.

Still, the legend says that sometime around 1500 AD, spiritual advisors or "medicine men" directed women who wanted male children to Mara. Blessed by shade in a land that had little, the palm grove Mecca also had sweet water with reputed supernatural properties. Mara, the family clinic of the ancient world. The hopeful migrations to the oasis must have succeeded. In the first year alone, the legend says, expectant mothers who visited the oasis were delivered of twenty nine male babies. They reportedly celebrated by planting one palm at the site for each infant boy. The trees they sowed grew tall, becoming guideposts visible over great distances. Only later did this same haven take on another type of maleness: a training ground for soldiers headed for oil-fueled battle in foreign deserts.

Thinned by fire in some places and trampled in others, the *Washingtonia* at Mara still summon visitors, murmuring veiled invitations.

We want sons, they might be saying. *Bring us sons.*

I walk the park service paths thinking of the pregnant women who may have blazed trails here. Strolling paths now paved and widened, I stop at a handrail to gaze into the hydric zone. This is the famous Oasis of Mara. This patch of sand and struggling palms. The formerly biodiverse, reputedly damp refuge is largely mesquite and *Washingtonia.*

Years later, on March 26, 2018, Mara was dealt another blow, when local resident and paroled arsonist George William Graham set fire to the palms. He played God with the remaining trees, taking a black BIC lighter to these besieged two-and-a-half acres. Several stressed, historic palms were destroyed along with a few other remnant plant species. Reminders of a greater spectrum of wildlife and once-vibrant lineage of ancient people went up in swirls of ash. Park rangers arrested Graham as he stuck around to watch the blaze.

ON DAY THREE I RISE BEFORE dawn to explore another oasis named for a tally of palms. Outside town, *Washingtonia* still grows naturally at springs and along fault lines in narrow canyons. That's the case at Fortynine Palms, a 1.5-mile walk from a trailhead not far from my motel. I make the short drive; I reach the lot at daybreak. The day's new sun throws beams over the facing ridge. Granite boulders shine beside the trail. Flakes of mica flash in the sand before my boots. Ridges along flanks of mountains shed light so that alluvial fans throw shadows. It's a brilliant morning.

Fortynine Palms strings before me, a green necklace. The oasis has a narrow hydric zone in a long, arid arroyo. Fresh water tickles among horsetails, maidenhair fern, willow, and cottonwood where a small bit of flow is enough to fill tiny, clear pools. Glassy surfaces are topped by gaggles of water striders. A buzz fills the air as life stirs with the sun. Hummingbirds divebomb in mating dances and zoom into blossoms on scattered stands of globe mallow. Gnatcatchers and orioles call, and the sweet scent of things growing permeates the morning.

With every step closer to the water source, I find more surprises. A stippled cluster of dog like prints of coyotes at mud rimmed pools, signs of a pack that's come and gone. Scat stuffed with bones and palm seeds. The California fan palm is not a date tree, but its small, black fruit still lures many creatures, including large mammals. Watch out, California and Gambel's quail—you could end up in the jaws of a hunting *Canis latrans.*

Moisture from below the surface seeps into my bootprints. It's a life-giving aspect of these narrow canyons, their wet backbones. Here, groundwater lurks beneath the barest skin of gravel and sand. Alternately, in the rainy months, too much water may rip through here— high, fast, and sudden. A storm far up the drainage may drench bedrock, then send snouts of muddy runoff through narrow, shotgun canyons. Flash floods roar and rip and uproot. They're the leading killer of California fan palms in tight, rock-bound arroyos. Not death by drying, as one might think, or the trampling of young palm pups under heavy hiking boots.

Rather, it's the screaming, wild, rain fed flood that upends elder palms and carries off seedlings, prying loose their shallow roots. Only the most sheltered and strongest survive these torrents that rise out of nowhere, churn through, and only spare trees if they're protected by a random boulder or arm of alluvial fan. The mud-floods leave silty scars on remaining trees, dozens of feet above ground. Look up in a palm canyon and you're bound to see high water marks far overhead.

Death by water in the desert: one of nature's greatest ironies.

As the day's heat mounts at Fortynine Palms, the music of birds fades. Insect drone takes over as bees of all sizes work the willow catkins. Two pair of quail pick at creosote and bob their way upcanyon, their loose-necked march mostly hidden beneath dry-channel canopy. I creep onto a boulder to let them pass. Three quail rely for safety on a fourth bird who perches on a pile of stones to serve as sentry. I hold my breath. The birds' jerky, searching movements take them past, apparently without seeing me, until they all turn without warning toward my right foot. Everything goes fine for a moment, until one bird reaches my boot, the sentry cries, and all four scatter like tossed dice.

The boot that scared them off looks harmless to me. Past it, however, I find something in the pink granite gravel that's shiny and not always so harmless—a single rifle shell, resting near my toes on the gravel bottomed wash. Luckily the shell is a casing, spent and empty. As I study it, a jet fighter stealth-flies like a harrier overhead, throwing shadow. The aircraft rips away with a roar.

WASHINGTONIA, IMPERATIVE TO LIFE in the Mojave, has as its doppelgänger the genus *Phoenix* in the Persian Gulf. Like the California fan palm, the highly cultivated, date bearing *Phoenix* needs full sun, heat, and scads of subsurface water. *Phoenix* has long brought wealth and status to its growers, because there's no end to what you can do with the tree. You can cut its fronds for shelter. You can weave its mature leaves into mats, screens, baskets, and crates. You can strip off its fruit clusters to prepare the fronds for brooms or weave palm fiber into skirts and sandals. The high-tannin date-fruit has cured everything from intestinal troubles to alcoholic intoxication through the ages.

Even if palm fruit doesn't cure hangover, as implied, the Phoenix tree of the Middle Eastern oasis stands for food, fiber, firewood. Survival for desert dwellers.

Ancient Mesopotamians encouraged *Phoenix* to grow at scattered hydric zones by planting them there and protecting the growth of young palm pups. Communities depended on the palms they had fostered. Honored in myth and mirage and a thousand Arabian nights, the date palm stood from time unknown in the wedge of land between the Tigris and Euphrates Rivers. Archaeological evidence of cultivars goes back to four thousand years before Christ. In a way, *Phoenix* is a messiah in its own right—abundant in its gifts, revered in the earliest bas-relief sculpture, exalted on the faces of antiquated coins.

A wonder tree. Own a palm, own the world.

Because the trees are critical to life both in and out of the oasis, they are strategic targets in times of war. *Phoenix* lore holds that in the 1824 siege of Suckna, a station on the caravan route between Mesopotamia and Central Syria, the conqueror Abdel-Gelil cut down more than forty thousand trees to compel the town to surrender. The campaign worked, and the scorched palm tactic has been used in many conflicts since to gain dominance over populations. For the Iraqi people, who have long led the world in date production, the much-harassed *Phoenix* has become a military Achilles' heel. Iraqis, wise and hardworking stewards of *Phoenix,* develop many of the most popular cultivars, including those bearing soft, sweet Halawy and Khadrawy fruits. Then, standing tall, holding the bread of life and unable to hide in an exposed landscape, the generous palm falls in mute capitulation when the enemy comes swinging sabers.

We in the West have done more than our share to destroy the palm in the Tigris-Euphrates. Iraq's forty million commercial trees had already come under attack in the 1980s' Iran-Iraq War. Sometime during the descent of allied forces in the 1991 Gulf War, numbers of palms registered just fifteen million. After September 11, 2001, Allied forces again invaded Iraq, albeit years later: US and British air strikes that began on March 20, 2003, and continued for three weeks coincided with and interrupted palm fertilization to Iraq's remaining ten million trees. Little has been written in Western news about the destruction of palms north of Baghdad in 2003, but newspapers from the area reported invading armies bulldozing farmers' trees to extract information about guerrilla insurgents. In 2005, Iraq's annual output of dates, usually twenty to thirty tons, was slim enough only to meet children's needs and provide dessert for growers' guests. In 2006, the same newspapers reported that any surviving trees were expected to be barren.

Exterminate the date palm, and you take a knife to the throats of its people. Kill the tree that rims the oasis, and you help bring Algerians, Moroccans, Tunisians, Egyptians, Arabians, Iranians, and Iraqis to their knees.

WAR FOUND MARA, too, coming in on the ancient native footpaths. After the shelter and open water drew miners, homesteaders, cattlemen, and the stage line, small outposts gradually coalesced into the village of Twentynine Palms. No longer the sacred destination for mothers desiring

to make sons, it drew the sons themselves. Most men arriving there had
either just returned from war or were about to go. Veterans of World War
I who'd suffered lung problems during the gassing in France came to the
clean, dry air to regain the power to breathe. Mara became life itself, with
long horizons and unbroken sunlight. Basins of rock and sand, a world
away from the mud and gloom of trench warfare and the dark, northern
forests of Europe, meant a return from the dark side of the moon.

When World War II loomed, the US military found the open skies
of Twentynine Palms ideal for glider instruction. The Navy expanded
that use into an auxiliary air station that later transferred to the Marine
Corps. The Semper Fi have live-fire trained there with no breaks since
1953. No rest for the warrior in either war or peace.

RETURNING TO TOWN, I'm jonesing for more hot-tub time and
maybe even an umbrella drink beside the swimming pool. Aglow from
hiking, I pass through the motel lobby and catch sight of a headline on
a newspaper in the media rack. Buying a paper, I detour to a plush chair
in the lobby. **TANK CREW FOUND.** The oversized font usually reserved for
presidential election upsets and fires that force evacuations now applies
to the team of men who trained right here only months ago.

When the Abrams was finally located, it was by Navy divers in twenty
feet of Euphrates River water. Somehow disoriented even after the sand-
storm cleared, the driver missed a turn and plunged off the end of an
unfinished bridge. The tank flipped, its turret and escape hatch shoving
into soft river mud. Trapped inside the Abrams, all four crew members
perished.

The Scotsman's pregnant wife is brave as she faces the reporters from
regional and national newspapers. "He loved his job," she says of her
deceased husband. "It totally fit him." She's showing huge composure
and keeping things brief. There are no hints about risk. Nothing about
the irony of death in a desert river. Reading her words, I want nothing
more than to find the communications officer. I rush to the swimming
pool to discover he's still at his post. He looks up from his math with a
quick smile. His face fills with the light of recognition.

I ask if he's heard about the tank crew. He has. The news has only
firmed his resolve to join his unit. His expression turns solemn. "I want

to go soon. I don't want to be like a prizefighter who trains day in and day out for two years and never gets to go in the ring."

The thought of him taking the blows suffered by pugilists, both in and out of the ring, hurts my heart. I try not to let my face show it as we fall into a tentative silence. It's a fool's desire to think that he might keep his wide-eyed, shining look. His young brain is still maturing, still growing its ability to reason. Only when he's lived to the ripe old age of twenty-six, I've read, will his nervous system be considered adult. Only then will he recognize life's warning lights, like the oil lamps on car dashboards that stop us from driving into danger. Risky behavior is especially attractive to a certain demographic, specifically Caucasian males under the age of twenty-five with high school educations or less. This young officer may qualify on all counts, but I won't ask. Neither is he about to bring it up.

He goes back to his math. I don't fold him in a protective embrace, but someone should. Should I pray? Or make a second wish? With my gaze on the motel palms again, I compose another eight-syllable blessing: *Please. Survive fire and water.*

He keeps his vigil with the books. The face of the pool shimmers. It's groundwater, Mara sustaining liquid, pumped out of soil and rock and into the desert air. Taking my place in the hot tub, within the hydric zone in this otherwise arid garden, I hold a vigil of my own. ⟡

2015 Finalist

Nathaniel Brodie

PROJECT DESCRIPTION

Entangled in the Land tells the story of the seven years I spent working on the Grand Canyon National Park Service Trail Crew. On one level this story is a bildungsroman: my search as a young man for intimacy and belonging, in both place and in romantic love, with all the accompanying tensions of wilderness and domesticity, wanderlust and rootedness, freedom and responsibility. A story of the man I was, the man the Canyon helped me become.

But this narrative of coming to know myself is inextricably entangled with the quest of coming to know the Grand Canyon—the Canyon is the true protagonist of this book, and I delve deeply into its natural and cultural histories, present(s), and possible futures. Of course, the Grand Canyon is not one thing but a million things: rivers, willows, peaks, valleys, condors, tourists, mines, dams, and so forth. Even taken as a whole, the Canyon is a mutable, epistemological dilemma; different from every perspective and to every person.

For this reason my personal narrative is stitched between some sixty concise essays, a mosaic of stories, ecologies, meditations, histories, images, and impressions. The Canyon that I came to know by working in its bitter colds and withering heats, shaping and dry-stacking its manifold rock, exploring it in person and on page, and alternately relishing and suffering its indifference, is my Canyon. But the story I tell of a young man searching for a place, for an understanding of both self and (lithic) other, is universal.

The Grand Canyon's most powerful quality may be its effect on perspective. By complicating and deepening the concept of perspective, of seeing and knowing a single place, of how one's personal geographies of experience, emotion, and development overlay a physical geography, this book may lead to deeper understandings of how we perceive other places, an especially meaningful effort in regard to our iconic, ecologically-fascinating, culturally-significant, and yet still unfathomed desert places.

The River That Will Remain

MY SETTLING BAG HIT THE EDDY current and inflated like a parachute. I had to use both hands to heave it out of the river and stagger it onto the small beach. The water inside the bag was turbid with suspended sediment. The silt would need a couple of hours to drift to the bottom of the bag, but I'd take what the last hour of daylight gave me—at least the larger grains would subside, and my water filter would last that much longer.

Scrambling up a series of sandstone ledges, I found a nice spot to sit: a bedrock backrest with a view of the wavering line where the waters of the Little Colorado River joined those of the Colorado River. The Little Colorado is usually an opalescent turquoise blue, milk-bright with dissolved travertine and limestone. But the rains from a few days earlier had rusted the color to that of an old ceramic pot, a few shades browner than the gray-green Colorado. The smaller river eased into the Colorado's corridor, but the two rivers didn't immediately merge; they simply ran, side by side, down the course of the Canyon. They'd maintain their distinct flows for a good half-mile before rapids disrupted them into unity. The meeting of any waters is mesmerizing to watch; especially so here, with the Little Colorado's suspended silt mushrooming into the silt-strained Colorado.

Silt-strained. From where I sat at the confluence, I was only sixty-one miles downstream of Glen Canyon Dam. Behind Glen Canyon Dam, the silt-laden, rusted-red Colorado River becomes Lake Powell. At the exact-if-ever-fluctuating spot where river slacks into reservoir the river drops its sediment load, just as the particles of suspended earth were drifting to the bottom of my settling bag. This is a load that wind, water, and humanity have scraped from 108,000 square miles of mostly arid, barren, and highly erodible land. Estimates on the exact annual size of this load range from 45 million tons to nearly 200 million tons, but even the lowest of these estimates is an enormous amount of sediment being deposited into the head of the impounded river. Some 180 miles later, when the dam releases the river from the bottom of the three-hundred-foot deep reservoir, a different river emerges: a green, bitterly cold, enslaved river, its soul having settled down with the silty coagulum burying the drowned contours of Glen Canyon.

The Glen Canyon Dam, completed in 1963, has wreaked havoc on downstream ecology. The seasonal flux of spring flood and winter ebb was replaced by a mechanical, anthropogenic rhythm: the dam now doles out the river in accordance with major metropolitan areas' electrical needs. Before the dam, the rise and ebb of floods would deposit and rearrange the river's sediment into ecologically important fluvial formations: sandbars, islands, beaches, backwaters. With the replenishing floods stifled by the dam and the sediment dropped at the top of the reservoir, the beaches and eddy sandbars are slipping away, grain by grain. No longer scoured by floods, the remaining beaches are increasingly impenetrable with tamarisk, Russian olive, and willow. No longer swept aside or rearranged by floods, the debris fans that form at the mouths of tributary canyons constrict the river, forming narrower, bonier rapids. Before the dam, the river could reach a high of eighty-five degrees Fahrenheit; the river is a now a consistently frigid forty-seven degrees—for this alone I hated it, how it spoiled one of life's greater pleasures: swimming in a summer-warmed river.

The dam's effects are geological as well as ecological. Before the dam, the melting of the Rocky Mountains' snowpacks sent spring floods raging through the Canyon. The highest recorded flood (in 1884) peaked at 300,000 cubic feet per second, or cfs (the dammed river now fluctuates between 7,000 to 30,000 cfs). And yet even that deluge is dwarfed by floods that ripped through the Canyon within the last 2 million years: the cyclic melting of the Quaternary Ice Ages produced flood after flood—some as large as one million cfs. These floods significantly contributed to the downcut topography of the Colorado Plateau; the geologist Wayne Ranney estimates that as much as half of the Grand Canyon's current depth—so, some 2,500 feet—occurred within this time. After all, the Colorado River did not carve the Grand Canyon by the steady rasp of sediment-laden waters abrading bedrock. A thick—in

some cases seventy-five-foot-thick—layer of silt, mud, and sediment
protects the bedrock from the river's scour. Only when the river swelled
in floods big enough to sweep away the sediment, and the giant boulders
suspended within the flood hammered the bared bedrock into clasts the
flood then whisked away, only then did the canyon deepen.

No more. The once diluvial Colorado River system is now constrained
by more than a hundred dams between headwaters and delta. The once
volatile river has been reduced, as the river guide and author Kevin
Fedarko has written, to "little more than a giant plumbing system" consigned to slake the thirst of some 30 million people. The river that carved
the Grand Canyon in a scant six million years has been fettered; the
canyon this river carved no longer deepens.

I HAD CROSSED THE LITTLE COLORADO RIVER and walked
upstream of the confluence to pump my drinking water, and not just
because the river was running thick. The Little Colorado's water is
some of the foulest in the Canyon: heavily mineralized, slimy, brackish,
stank. Jack Sumner, one of Powell's crewmates on his first trip down the
Canyon in 1869, found it "a lothesome little stream, so filthy and muddy
that it fairly stinks ... as disgusting a stream as there is on the continent
... half of its volume and two-thirds of its weight is mud and silt. [It
was little but] slime and salt." A hundred years' worth of human efflu-
via: battery acid, car oil, tires, trash, as well as traces of one of the worst
radioactive spills in US history, when 100 million gallons of radioactive
water were accidently released into a major tributary in 1979, has done
little to improve its flavor.

But honestly, even though it begins as Rocky Mountain snowmelt,
by the time it reaches the Canyon, the Colorado River's water isn't all
that much more palatable. I pumped a liter and took a sip. Alkaline,
almost curdled. The rim of my bottle was gritty; I could feel the grains
of rock rasp my tongue, the sand grind my teeth. Despite the dam, the
Colorado through the Canyon is by no means devoid of silt. According
to Gwendolyn L. Waring, author of *A Natural History of the Intermountain
West: Its Ecological and Evolutionary Story*, the river below the dam still
conveys some 12 million tons of silt a year. Twelve million tons of silt
still makes for a raspy river. Much of the silt comes from the Pariah River,

which enters the Colorado hyper-saturated with the pink, hematite-rich soils of Bryce Canyon. Waring claims that the Pariah, a Paiute word meaning "muddy" or "elk water," has "carried greater concentrations of suspended sediment than any other river in North America; concentrations of up to 2 pounds of sediment per quart." The Little Colorado supplies a significant amount of sediment; the rest comes from the park's hundreds of tributary canyons. And thus a drink of the river, despite the twist of the mouth at the taste, is a desert communion: the dolomites and mudrocks of Nankoweap or Kwagunt basins, having clouding into the Colorado, now billow into my bloodstream.

The Southwest's intense monsoon thunderstorms play an integral role in the conveyance of tributary silt. For those few wet months, floods and debris flows—ranging from 3,500 to 10,600 cfs and, at least once this century as high as 35,314 cfs—race down the tributaries, scorching the river its namesake red. Flush with runoff, again the river moves the wasted continent to the sea. You open your eyes underwater and it's black as a cave. Like being buried alive.

Yet because of repressed river flow, most of this tributary sediment settles to the riverbed shortly downstream of the tributary canyons. Since 1996 the various federal agencies managing the dam and river—mainly the Bureau of Reclamation, US Fish and Wildlife Service, and the National Park Service—have been experimenting with short-duration, high-volume dam releases (aka "high-flow experiments," or HFEs) designed to mobilize these thick mantles of sand and sediment in hopes that when the flood subsides, the mobilized sand will have replenished downstream beaches and riparian areas. As of 2017 they'd conducted six such experiments, with no flood larger than 45,000 cfs. The latest tactic, now part of the Glen Canyon Dam Adaptive Management Program, is to strategically time the high flows with the episodic flooding of tributaries, as when, in a three-month, end-of-monsoon-season span in 2012, the Paria River debouched at least 538,000 metric tons of sand into the Colorado River.

However, according to a 2011 USGS report, the relation "among sand supplied from tributaries, short-term sand enrichment in the Colorado River, sand transport during HFEs, sand transport between HFEs during normal operations, and the resultant sand mass balance" is complex, and delicate, and "uncertainties still remain about downstream impacts of water releases from Glen Canyon Dam." For example, the experimental floods may have had a role in the 800 percent increase in the catch rates of rainbow trout—the endangered humpback chub's main predator—at the confluence between 2007 and 2009. On a wider scale, the question remains whether tributaries even supply enough sand "to provide the elevated suspended-sediment concentrations needed to build and also maintain sandbars."

Because of this, environmentalists have urged the Bureau of Reclamation to install a slurry pipe that would inject reservoir sediment back into the river, though the bureau has indicated no more willing-ness to do this than to install a native-fish-friendly device that pulls warm water from the surface of the reservoir though the penstocks. They have valid reasons: sediment released from Lake Powell will only further reduce the already diminished capacity of Lake Mead, a far more stra-tegic reservoir, and warmer water, while bad for trout, might increase the populations of other voracious warm-water nonnative fishes. Still, the bureau has been historically, notoriously recalcitrant concerning anything other than the Glen Canyon Dam's main purpose as a "cash register" dam, and even getting them to conduct some of the high-flow experiments required litigation.

So it goes with the Colorado River these days; as Marc Reisner put it in his classic book *Cadillac Desert:* "The Colorado's modern notoriety ... stems not from its wild rapids and plunging canyons but from the fact that it is the most legislated, most debated, and most litigated river in the entire world." Though there is a great and necessary deal of coopera-tion over this miracle of a desert river "resource," scarcity and complexity breed conflict, and often enough it's the Bureau of Reclamation versus the National Park Service versus the Fish and Wildlife Service versus the Navajo Nation versus conservation organizations; urban Phoenicians versus pima cotton farmers versus whitewater rafters; "upper-basin" states versus "lower-basin" states versus the federal government; on and on, all the parties with their own vested interests, competing values, institutional ideologies, and narrative blinders.

And beyond the tangle of acronyms, abstractions, and differing philosophies is the squat, concrete reality of the dam. So, too, for all the ways our individual and cultural conceptions allow us to see or not see the Grand Canyon, and as much as it may be the most staggering, unknowable, sublime phenomenon that I have ever experienced, the Canyon is still rock, and wind, and river. I was born sixteen years too late to have experienced the Canyon before the dam. I couldn't—can't—see the native fish slipping toward extinction. I haven't yet spent enough years on the river to witness the beaches waning to nothing, the rapids choking with boulders. There is only so much my mind can bear to read about acre-feet allocations, fluvial geomorphology, and adaptive management programs. But every year, as the monsoons waned, I watched brown-green veins more frequently marble the firebrand red until, in time, the entire river flowed that sullen, incarcerated green.

Conversely, during those months when the tributaries are flashing, turning the river brown, or during those rare, brief days of high-flow experiments, one understands that the central miracle of the Grand Canyon is the staggering amount of material that the river is capable of conveying. It's so obvious that it's commonly disregarded, or slips past without notice, but the exposed and spreading rock is not the Grand Canyon: the Canyon is the absence of that rock. The Canyon is a lacuna—a gap, a segment of earth torn from its surroundings, the thousand cubic miles of rock that the river has excavated. And not merely the iconic gorge itself—in what the geologist Clarence Dutton dubbed "the great denudation," strata a mile thick was removed from the top of the Grand Canyon region. An entire landscape, gone. The Moenkopi layer, gone. Chinle layer, gone. The Moenave, Kayenta, Navajo, Templecap, Carmel, Dakota, Tropic, Wahweap, Kaiparowits, Wasatch, Brian Head—almost 200 million years' worth of sedimentary deposition—gone. The arterial river flume sluiced the broken landscapes to the Sea of Cortez. Wells sunk along the river's delta have penetrated eighteen thousand feet of alluvial fill without hitting bedrock. Fifty thousand cubic miles of sediment may lie buried under the Gulf of California. In time, that material will be subducted and reabsorbed into the hot crust of the earth, and, in even greater scales of time, again rise to the surface as new earth.

And yet, for a geologic gasp, no more sediment disgorges into the gulf. None.

In the fathomless reaches of geologic time, a few centuries' or millennias' lack of silt won't affect the tectonic cycle in the slightest. And that's part of the magic of the Grand Canyon: all I had to do to feel, if not hope, with at least a comforting sense of context, was to look around me, press my bare palms against that unbearably ancient rock, slide my bare feet in that cold, indifferent water. I may mourn that I'll never get to see a 200,000 cfs flood deepening the Canyon, or that I'll never get to sit at the confluence of the free-flowing San Juan River and the free-flowing Colorado River and watch the sediment of one curl like spiral galaxies into the deep space of the other, I find some small, fatalistic comfort in the fact that the dam is a temporary barrier, that the river, as Robinson Jeffers put it, is a "heart-breaking beauty [that] will remain when there is no heart to break for it."

My water bottles full, I poured the remaining water in my settling bag into the shallows. The force of the water plumed sand into suspension, some of which settled back to the bottom, some of which was whisked away by the eddy. I watched the gauzy ribbons of sediment flow past, allowed myself to fancy that they made the main current to be carried down the river's length to the waters of Lake Mead, where the individual grains will again succumb to their minuscule gravities and fall, slowly, to the bottom. ᢙ

(A version of this essay first appeared in *Hawk and Handsaw: Journal of Creative Sustainabilty*, Volume 8 (2016).)

2015 Finalist

Maya Kapoor

PROJECT DESCRIPTION

As human populations in the American Southwest grow at rates faster than anywhere else in the U.S.—in some cases, at twice the average national rate—I am drawn to writing about species whose lives and ecology are inextricably intertwined with those of humans. I hope to add to desert literature by writing about desert landscapes through the lens of urban ecology. Urbanization of desert ecosystems is a topic covered in academic and journalistic writing, but as of yet neglected in desert literature, despite its growing importance for human and natural systems. From rare desert fish captively bred to be "wild," to urban pests that thrive in desert oases like Tucson—the city where I live—desert life forms challenge my understanding of what *wild* means at every ecological scale.

At the same time, I have been challenged in my understanding of wildness by a chronic illness—epilepsy—that I developed only recently. Initially conceived as science writing, this project has been structured by my physical and logistical limitations, leading me also to become interested in ideas of self-identity tied up in cultural constructions of the West. Begun as an exploration of under-appreciated and uncharismatic life forms of the Sonoran desert, this writing project has become a paired interrogation of the ecological and cultural meanings of *wild* and has taken on the form of science writing scaffolded by memoir.

My project is a nonfiction essay collection that is a mix of science writing and memoir. The collection focuses on often overlooked life forms from the Sonoran desert—the uncharismatic or under-appreciated species existing in marginal spaces where the human and natural complicate one another's identities. Each organism's story is a window into questions of what it means for something to be wild or urban (or wild and urban) in the Anthropocene.

THREE ESSAYS

Counting Cover

THE PATCH OF GROUND OF INTEREST is one meter squared, about half the size of a twin mattress, a quadrat measured by the placement of a white PVC frame I have been carrying around all afternoon. Sometimes squatting, sometimes standing, I stare into the frame. I am recording plant cover.

A clump of blue grama grass, its seed heads curled like commas, occupies 10% of the quad. The delicate red stem and leaves of a goosefoot fit under a dime: 0.05%. Between the plants lies silky soil, which gets its own cover measurement: 5%. I notice dried-mud termite casings sheathe last year's grass stems, stretching up a few inches before breaking off and eroding in the wind. When I move, two-inch-long black and yellow grasshoppers spook into the air, then swoop back down to settle on the ground a few feet away. Black Butte—too small to bother conquering, too big to meander up—hulks on the desert floor, marking the northern edge of this central New Mexican wildlife refuge. When I straighten and take a moment to stretch my back, I see contrails feathering blue sky.

The field biologist's piecemeal way of focusing on one detail, then another, noting colors from the corner of my eye, identifying plants from just a hint of form in the distance, is how I learned to love the desert so intimately. It took a while—I did not grow up in a desert, and when I moved to Albuquerque from a summer botany job in a tiny verdant town in Montana, the landscape looked bleak and beat to me.

The mountains have been blowing out birthday candles all month. The hot wind frays my nerves; even the sight of soil swirling across the highway irritates me on weekend drives to Albuquerque. Today I am wearing long pants and an old gray sweatshirt to work. If I take the sweatshirt off, I shiver. I leave it on and sweat. There have been rare days in field seasons past when it snowed and my fingers numbed as I tried to poke out a 2.5 or .05 or even a cover of .01 with a stylus. More frequently,

I have lain under the truck to find shade during my lunch break, staring out between its tires at a shadowless land.

Cactus pads scattered here and there make me nervous—I sat on one once—but generally my day proceeds smoothly. When one quad is done, I move on to another. As the sun moves, I move, orbiting quads, keeping computer and plants in my shadow. The information I am collecting is for a long-term data set begun eight years ago, before I even arrived in the desert. There is no foreseeable end to this project.

This work can be meditative—shutting out the rest of the world to focus on slow-growing things. But for every prophet in the desert finding enlightenment, there must be hundreds of field biologists merely bored, hot, sunburnt, and hungry, or just plain lost. Still, the desert gets under my skin. When I learn a new plant. When a mountain lion dashes across the road in front of the truck. When an errant herd of feral oryx (whose ancestors were brought here from Africa in the 1960s by the chairman of the New Mexico Game Commission, then illegally released into the wild) appears nervously in the distance.

Mornings, I step outside with a mug of tea and watch the sunrise. The huge expanse of sky all around me glows a flaming orange. Trees, houses, and mountains are backlit into obscurity. In such moments the desert feels immeasurable.

I am distracted from my accounting this afternoon by a stinkbug trundling through the quadrat. I know I will not do this work much longer. After a while, careful repetition exhausts me. Consider this: it has gotten to the point where I recognize not just species, but individual plants as they grow within their quads from season to season.

Really, I never meant to spend a quarter of my life in the desert. To be fair, I've left several times already: for a summer in Montana measuring Douglas-firs and eating huckleberries; for a couple of field seasons in Costa Rica; for a sojourn along the Appalachian Trail. But I kept coming back to the Southwest. I have worked as an environmental educator, a National Park Service interpreter, a volunteer backcountry ranger, and, again and again, as a botanist measuring plants. I think often about escaping to moister climates, to places populated with what I consider to be real trees, trees cloaked in dripping moss, or to coastlines with tide pools to explore. But my forward momentum evaporates in the dry desert wind.

I remember suddenly how at 23 I was making my way from North Carolina to Oregon when I took an impulsive detour to Las Cruces. Now, almost a decade later, I pause from rinsing a soapy mug in the kitchen and contemplate the creosote I see through the window. I will leave after the winter field season.

When I can no longer abide counting plants, I start writing as a means of escape. But what comes out of me are cottonwoods tracing dry rivers, prickly pears feeding young rabbits, yuccas cradling high-country snow. What comes out of me is desert vegetation.

My grandparents told my mother when she was a child that if she swallowed orange seeds a tree would grow inside her; I must have swallowed entire wildflower mixes. When I take trips, I look out plane windows to calculate covers for mountains, rivers, farms. I guess at the names of vaguely familiar foliage in unfamiliar towns. As with many in the Southwest, I develop terrific crow's-feet. When I smile, deep lines reach from the corners of my eyes toward my hairline. I never did wear sunglasses in my early years as a desert botanist. They changed the color of the leaves too much.

The desert is engraved on my skin. It shapes my language. It highjacks my imagery. These days I sit at my kitchen table drinking tea and typing. I am still counting cover, in a way, measuring the extent of the desert inside of me.

❧

Release

I HAVE JUST HOOKED MY FIRST CATCH at 33 after a lifetime of recreational pacifism. Kneeling on the sandy gravel beside the lake, I pin the fish to the ground with my left hand and grip the knife in my right. I pause to remind myself what comes next.

I know, in theory, how to get the head off a fish. And bobber fishing, the kind you do on a sleepy Sunday by the side of a little lake, is not exactly *A River Runs Through It* material. But now that I actually have a fish in my hands, I hesitate, a cold wind raising goose bumps on my arms. I have no idea what I am doing.

Arizonans love to fish. Arizonans love to fish to the point of diverting creeks, moving earth, and building hatcheries. We love fishing so much, we truck fish to our waterways and dump them in, just so we can catch them again. Game fish like brown and rainbow trout flourish in Arizona's built water systems, including reservoirs, urban lakes, and streams. Brown trout are a European species; rainbows are from tributaries of the Pacific Ocean. The native trout of Arizona—Gilas and Apaches—are all but extinct these days, due largely to competition, inbreeding, and predation by browns and rainbows introduced for sport. Apache trout, listed as threatened by state and federal agencies, is the state fish of Arizona.

This fishing trip is one of my many efforts to make sense of the complicated history of Arizona fisheries. The more I try to understand fishing in Arizona—which, granted, is fishing in the desert—the less it makes sense to me. I have a master's degree in biology. I think about Arizona fish like an ecologist. But our fisheries history reflects more of an angler perspective, and so I'm trying to learn how to fish.

I huddle over my fish with my back to the sun. It is February, and Rose Canyon Lake, in the Catalina Mountains north of Tucson, is peaceful. Young ponderosas and manzanitas lean in from the edges of the canyon; cattails fringe the water. Patches of snow glimmer in shade and sheets of ice cover shallows. During the May to October high season, anglers looking for fishing spots crowd the water's edge, but this morning I count only three other groups. Four men in army fatigues heckle each other on the dock across the lake. Once in a while their voices carry over. They tease one another about the size of their catches ("You call that a fish? That's not a fish! I don't know what that is!") and the relative hopelessness of their fishing techniques. To our left are two peaceable old men in dirty leather cowboy hats. "You never take more than your catch allowance, right?" They drawl at us. "That wouldn't be right." Around the sweep of Rose Canyon Lake to our right, too far away to hear, three young Hispanic fathers and their little boys fish and shoot a BB gun at the air. When nothing is biting, the children giggle and chase each other in the sun.

The most natural motion seems to be sawing a line under the fish's fins like I am slicing a loaf of bread. "Do it fast—don't saw!" Jess, the woman teaching me to fish, reminds me that a fast decapitation is a humane decapitation. In theory, this fish is already dead, but there is a small chance that snapping its back didn't actually kill it. Lacking a trout-sized guillotine, I hold my breath and push.

Brown trout always sounded to me like the name of a muddy animal consigned to silted ponds, something inconspicuous, something named in opposition to a rainbow trout, its prettier, more popular sister. But my brown trout is beautiful, with black spots like a tiger's on skin that gleams silver in the sun. The spots in a horizontal row on its white belly are magenta, the flash of flesh under its gills crimson. What's more, my trout is surprisingly soft under my cold palm, its skin smooth against my own. Somehow, I had expected a fish to be something that felt already dead—something rough, cold, stiff. Something that came out of the freezer at a grocery store. What I feel under my hand is taut skin binding lithe muscle into form. I don't want to admit this to the others in my group, but I am enchanted by the silkiness of fish under my fingertips.

For me, cutting the head off a fish is a curiosity, a cultural experience. For this fish, getting decapitated is an inevitability, part of a closed system. This fish is getting her head cut off because that's what she was raised for by the Arizona Department of Game and Fish. If I didn't do this, someone else would. Trout never last long in Rose Canyon Lake. My trout is part of Arizona's giant angler economy. People in Arizona spend over $800 million on fishing-related expenses a year. During warmer weather, wildlife managers drop fish into Rose Canyon Lake on average about once a month, and just as quickly, anglers pull them out again. This lake isn't a place where anything like a renewable fish population lives; this lake is managed for what is called put-and-take fishing. Hundreds of eleven-inchers get thrown into the lake on a pre-published schedule, along with the occasional incentive fish—the really huge trout, the giants bred at the state hatcheries that make the fishing more exciting. With my $63 non-resident fishing permit crumpled into the back pocket of my jeans, I am a part of this economy now too.

I sit back on my heels, wipe the knife on my thigh, and grin at the fish head gazing up from the ground. Jess is not impressed. When I landed my catch, she had noticed my gameness for doing my own dirty work and handed over her knife. But then Jess noticed how, at the last second, without realizing it, I clenched my eyes tightly and averted my face as far to the right as I could without severing my own head. She warns against this impulse. "You've got to be careful with closing your eyes—sometimes the body jumps. You could cut your hand." Still, where there was one whole fish there are now two pieces lying in the dirt. I gaze proudly at my bloody handiwork. I do not tell Jess that the first time I opened a can of sardines I ended up needing stitches.

In decapitating a fish I am participating in a quintessential American pastime, the catching and eating of a meal. This isn't just so I can text my siblings pictures of bloody fish guts while they are at work. I want to have the full fishing experience, to take responsibility for my catch by turning it into dinner. How else can I understand the culture of fishing, where this kind of thing is normal? Plus, to be honest, I really want to eat some fish.

One of my neighbors didn't understand why I had never been fishing before the Rose Canyon Lake trip. He told me his grandfather had taken him fishing when he was a kid. I explained my grandfather had been a vegetarian.

"What are you," he asked, "Pentecostal or something?"

"No—" Were Pentecostals vegetarian? I had a vague idea they did something with snakes. Did their worldview of, as I recalled, petting and talking to snakes, extend to all creatures? "We're Hindu." Later, I was told by more knowledgeable friends that vegetarianism is not a Pentecostal tradition, but it is a Seventh Day Adventist one, and perhaps that was what my neighbor meant.

Vegetarianism is also a Hindu tradition, and we get that fish are animals. To be sure, my family is extremely open-minded about personal interpretations of religious traditions; my parents love a good steak. Nonetheless, as of my fishing trip I have been a vegetarian on and off, but mostly on, for 21 years. But I decided I was willing to relax my food rules if it would bring me closer to understanding why we have this fishing industry at all, in such an arid land. Nothing was off the table.

"Put the knife in *here*," Jess says, indicating the fish's cloaca, the single orifice through which the fish, until recently, conducted all digestive and reproductive business. "Then hold the knife at an angle and cut up." I hold the fish on her side and slide the knife into her flesh, then push it away from my abdomen and through her sternum. My fish falls open like a book; together, Jess and I read the chapters of her life. "It's female," Jess says, digging the fish's ovaries out from where they lie underneath the digestive system. "Look—full of eggs." Jess hands me a translucent orange sac, long and skinny like a tiny hot dog, crammed with little shining beads. "She's early to be this fertile. It's only February." The eggs are immature. My fish was a juvenile when she swallowed the hook. "Here's her liver, I don't know what it's doing up *here*," Jess says, indicating a dark, smooth organ. I hold the liver in my fingers; it glistens in the sun. The stomach is a rubbery white tube shaped like a flower on one end. The swim bladder is deflated, barely visible against the fish's back. After I've removed everything else, I run the back of my thumb nail up the fish's spine from bottom to top the way I have seen Jess do with other fish, scraping out the last of the congealed blood. There. My fish is clean— minus the dirt, gravel, and dead grass pasted all over it, of course. The first time I saw Jess gut a fish she moved so fast that when she was done and all that was left was smooth white meat, muscles still twitched under iridescent skin.

I ask Jess, who in her day job is a native fish expert at the University of Arizona, if the remnant of the natural creek feeding Rose Canyon Lake harbors native fish species. It does not. The lake is a reservoir, and prior to its construction, trout did not swim this mountain. Yet even out here, in high mountains looming above the Sonoran Desert north of Tucson, we have built a lake and put in fish. We have put in roads, walkways, docks. We have added crayfish, built houses, shot some animals, raised and released others. All this, so I can go fishing.

It's easy for me to vilify my trout. To look around at this whole scene, this whole system, and reject it. To be suspicious of a fishing economy based upon releasing brown and rainbow trout into artificial water bodies like Rose Canyon Lake, and into natural water bodies elsewhere in the state. Environmental economists talk about existence value, how something can matter to people even if they never get to see it. Polar bears have existence value to me. So do elephants. On a local level, so does native biodiversity. I am impressed by the tough trout formed by our capricious waterways, by their strength of body, by their endurance. Whether or not I ever see Apache or Gila trout in the wild, I want to know they are out there, streaking through clear water, stalking caddis flies, leaning into currents. I think about the approximately two million hatchery trout released in Arizona in the previous year. Many of those fish were released into bodies of water that were once home to native trout. There may not be native fish swimming around the creek I can hear upstream of where I sit flicking entrails into cattails. There may never have been. Because I am part of Arizona's recreational fishing economy, ghosts of native fish nip at the edges of my conscience, nonetheless.

The thing is, out here on the lake, the story is more complex than conservationists versus anglers. My trout was grown and released to do more than entertain me. Unless I manage to catch another, my trout cost me $63. My catching another seems unlikely, given that I feel guilty even looking at the live earthworms Jess brought and I am not having the slightest luck with any of her florescent artificial baits, not even the sparkly pink one, or the fake salmon eggs laced with something called "SEXattract." Arizona pays for its native fish conservation plans through the sale of fishing licenses. In other words, the market for fishing permits to catch fish like mine is what supports the captive breeding and reintroduction of rare native species.

The fishing permit I purchased from Game and Fish is funding fish management efforts that will in theory someday lead to being able to fly fish native trout in native streams—and not just stocked native trout, which are already available in a few places in Arizona. Naturally reproducing populations of native trout you hike to in the forested mountains far from town, then catch out of cold, fast creeks, using a lifetime of patience and skill.

Before I wrap my fish in a plastic bag, Jess instructs me to wash it off. Holding the fish open in my palms like a holy book I dip it gently in the lake, cursing earnestly as my hands ache from cold. I swish the dirt off the fish, then toss the fish to the shallows to keep it cool. It sits on top of the ice. I rub my benumbed fingertips and look around for something non-fishy to eat. Then I rebait my hook with a smorgasbord of fish treats—artificial maggots, salmon eggs, something that looks like orange play-dough. To catch one fish and kill it wasn't the point of learning to fish; that would have been making a gesture. I am genuinely trying to adopt a hobby, at least for a day.

If I do somehow catch another fish, I would like to release it. In fishing terms, catch-and-release means you let the fish go after you pull it in. It means gently pulling out the hook, which ideally clings to the fish's mouth, and watching the fish flick its muscular tail and disappear underwater. To the part of me that isn't totally sure about this whole fishing adventure, release means giving up my idea of the perfect conservation plan for Arizona's native fish. It means finding a realistic way for people to live in the landscape, not just near it.

I look around the lake. One of my companions sits on a log, hunching slightly in the cold. Yesterday she strolled up just as the sun was setting, baited her first hook, hurled unrelenting verbal abuse upon any fish that might be listening in the lake—it sounded like she was saying, "Get on my hook, fishes!" but with different nouns—and promptly landed a trout. Today, she is content to sit in the sun smoking silently, indifferent to the outcome of her fishing. A couple of other women shift on the shore nearby, casting and pulling, moving with the sun. Jess moves between us, checking on technique, giving us pointers, and answering our questions. "Aim for right next to that big log," she tells me. "If I were a trout, that's where I would live." Occasionally she wanders back to her own rod, which is propped up on a forked branch she dug into the ground, to see if anything is tugging on the line.

I carry my rod to a flat spot on the water's edge, look around to make sure no other humans are close enough for me to hook, and snap out a cast that smacks the water a few feet away instead of arcing toward the center of the lake. Swearing luridly—I seem to have gotten that part of fishing down—I turn my reel, bringing in the hook so I can try again.

I am not sure, as I stand watching the water, waiting for a pull on my line telling me something has bitten, whether this—this afternoon of sunlit ripples, of relaxing with good company, of breezes carrying cattail fluff, of jays calling from the trees, this moment of snowy lake water, this escape from my responsibilities in town to breathe mountain air, this Sunday of men taking time with their friends and sons, whether all of this—can be both the cause and the solution for Arizona's native trout decline. But I am willing to consider that it might. At least for today, I am willing to release my ideas of what conservation should look like and consider that maybe it really looks like this.

❧

Euphorbia

WHEN THE OLD IMPULSE OVERTAKES ME, I tear stems from plants, watch sap bead out, the color of Elmer's glue, warm and sticky. I stuff euphorbias in my pockets. Back home, I flatten them under books on my desk or my nightstand. I forget them for days. And then I don't want to look at them again because they are crushed. I pull withered leaves from under my reading and sand-grain-sized seeds bounce onto the floor. I go out and collect more euphorbias. I do this because I am a recovering botanist.

I learned to identify species of *Euphorbia* subgenus *Chamaesyce* on overgrazed Chihuahuan desert in New Mexico. As late afternoon slanted into deep evening in a silent field station herbarium smelling of dried grasses and old books, I read through a heavy botanical key, the euphorb section, again and again. Bending over a microscope where fragments of plants lay in circles of light, I studied vegetation that bled white and blushed red and sometimes had teeth or hair or wings. The out-of-print Martin & Hutchins creaked along its spine when I pressed it open. Slowly I deciphered the language of floral body parts.

To follow a key is to have faith that my questions have answers I am capable of finding. Is this membrane smooth or jagged? Is this flower male or female? What species are you? It is parsing a thing by way of its smallest details. To follow a botanical key is to believe naming is a power-ful act, that names convey knowledge. Why do you grow this way? Why in this season, this place? Will you be here next year? Answers require names. Reading the euphorb key, shuffling through cabinets stacked with stiff plants reclining on great sheets of cardstock, I found order in mys-tery, evidence of a hidden elegance to things. I put the key away years ago but keep picking euphorbias.

In desert washes outside of town, I find euphorbias in ankle-high clumps, bright green, reddish about the edges, sprouting millimeters-long leaves from tentacled branches. Fruits hang pendulously late in summer, and yet what looks like a flower is not a flower; it's a clus-ter of male flowers around a single female flower, and all of them are naked, and what I thought were petals are pillowy white bracts. Who will pollinate you this way? To work through botanical keys is to trust the evolution of floral oddities, to see how with familiarity comes understanding.

Euphorbias are a sign of degraded desert. This means I see them everywhere. Under my car at the trailhead. In the dirt beside a lamp post in town. On beat-up highway verges, beneath creosote bushes, in my neighbor's dried-out yard. We travel in similar circles. Always, this compulsion to peel leaves and stems away, to see latex sap, to say—I *do* know you. Organisms of margins, euphorbias teach me, in the desert, that nothing is wild; in the city, that everything is. Poisoning livestock, feeding solitary bees, growing on tumbled earth and backyard xeriscape, euphorbias confound such romantic distinctions.

They are not charismatic plants. I went on a desert plant walk with a group of amateur botanists where we spent the day naming every plant we saw. Everyone ignored the euphorbias.

But I cannot dismiss euphorbias as weeds. They grow everywhere I do. And I prefer my plants strange.

Euphorbias grow spreading canopies; walking in waterless arroyos, I see shade—puddles of it, pooling dark and cool. Whisker-thin ants dash through dappled light, between circles cast by bunched leaves. The ants harvest fruits in their euphorbia groves. They eat sugary elaiosomes from seeds, then toss what's left in ant compost piles, where new euphorbias grow. I stand in the sun watching, wiping sweat from my neck. I worry euphorbias function at scales inaccessible to me. Is this a membrane or a mountain? How long have you been here, working out connections? This is not what I meant when I said I was looking for a tree.

I used to think naming was a form of ownership. I saw scientist and specimen, separated by a microscope. Over time, I learned that naming is committing to a relationship, is acknowledging community. Is identifying true intent. In naming you, I reveal myself. Now I see myself and euphorbias, living in the same landscape, and I am far outnumbered.

On my way to work I glimpse clumps of euphorbias, flourishing at sidewalk's edge. These days I work indoors at a computer. Because I no longer wrestle with specific epithets, no longer despair over the exact form of a plant's hairs, no longer cross my eyes wondering if tiny leaves are shaped more like hearts or triangles, I look away. I curl my fingers in my pocket. I resist the urge to steal, to keep, to flatten. I don't have the tools to name you anymore, and it would take a lifetime of study to understand you. But euphorbia—I know you. It's me. We are here together. ∽

(Originally published at terrain.org.)

2015 Finalist

Caroline Treadway

PROJECT DESCRIPTION

I propose to write a collection of essays, with photographs, about ants in the desert southwest. *Step On This: Desert Ants* would bridge the divide between entomologist and layperson, bringing these tiny creatures to life through narrative and imagery.

I will continue fieldwork with Dr. Gary Alpert and Stefan Cover on the Navajo Reservation, in the Grand Canyon and the Sky Islands of the southwestern U.S. and northern Mexico. The desert southwest is home to a high diversity of ant species.

Ants are one of the most successful and widespread organisms on the planet. They live in cities and suburbia. They live in the arctic and the jungle. E.O. Wilson writes that the body mass of all ants is equal to the body mass of all humans on the planet. Humans constantly seek common ground with ants, trying to learn from their decentralized intelligence. Ants are at once human, yet inhuman.

From above, ants all look similar. Up close, their lives are rich sagas that rival any science fiction novel. There is Polyergus, the slave-making ant, which raids Formica nests, steals their young, and raises them as their own. There are gardening ants, which eat fungus they cultivate deep in the earth. There are Honeypot ants, which use individuals as food banks, fatten them with nectar and sip from them in tough times. There are Army ants, which are blind, but coordinate massive night raids that have inspired human military tactics for centuries. There is Odontomacchus, which has the fastest hair-triggered jaws in the natural world, exerting a force of over 300 times its body weight on its victim. Imagine walking around all day with your jaws open 180 degrees until you found something to eat!

Once people begin to learn about ants, they usually get hooked. But entomologists are often too obsessed and too busy to write about their work for the general public. As a result, we miss out on the fascinating world at our feet.

Love and Botany—a Work in Progress

I'M SITTING AT A PIZZA JOINT in Durango, Colorado, with Arnold Clifford. The place is empty and dark. A small TV hums overhead. After a long stare out the window, Arnold faces me, puffs up his chest and says, "I've been thinking. Life might be good for you on the Reservation. Would you marry me?"

A hot breeze slams the screen door shut and washes the smell of fresh pizza over us.

I picture us together, standing on the desert I would inherit. I'm wrapped in blankets. The wind whips my long hair. A pack of wild horses roams against a fiery sunset. I would be a queen by Navajo standards. I'd have a tribe.

I've never felt like I belonged anywhere. And I've never been proud of my roots.

"I'll give you two years to think about it," Arnold says, avoiding my eyes.

❧

ARNOLD DIGS INTO THE PALE, GYPSUM hillside with his graceful, brown fingers. He loosens a dead stalk and holds it up to the sky. He squints at it through scratched Harley Davidson glasses. "Pretty sure this is a new species of *Phacelia*," he says solemnly, almost reverent. Then he breaks into a grin revealing a few missing teeth.

He wraps the specimen in a white plastic grocery bag from City Market. His eyes sparkle, criminally. We hike back to the truck. His red Mazda pick-up is parked on an anonymous, 4×4 road near the northern border of the Navajo Reservation. The only landmark is an old Chevy convertible, half-eaten by desert, a few miles back. Monument Valley, 30 miles southwest, makes faded purple cutouts on the horizon. The landscape feels more like Mars than Utah.

The Navajo Reservation spans almost 27,000 square miles of desert in Utah, New Mexico and Arizona. Home to over 250,000 people, the Navajo Nation is the largest reservation in the United States. Bigger than the state of West Virginia, the area remains relatively unexplored by scientists. It's one of the last botanical frontiers in the United States.

"People think everything out here has been found, but you just have to keep looking," Arnold says. "The more barren an outcropping is, the more likely there's something really special growing on it."

Arnold has discovered over 25 plant species in the southwest. Sixty more await consideration. He's made state records in Arizona, New Mexico, Colorado and Utah. Several plants have been named after him including *Senecio cliffordii* (Clifford's groundsel) and *Astragalus cliffordii* (Clifford's milk-vetch).

Arnold, 50 years old, lives with his mother and father in Beclabito, N.M. Arnold's personal herbarium is a makeshift hut of cinderblocks, corrugated metal and broken windows that sits on a sandy plot he inherited from his grandmother. The roof is partly caved. Gray light filters into the musty room. The corners are thick with cobwebs. Archaeological treasures line the windowsills and every available surface.

Hundreds of moldy cardboard boxes are stacked to the ceiling. They contain more than 100,000 plant specimens. Each has been found, pressed, glued to herbarium paper, and labeled in Arnold's neat script.

Arnold's grandmother, Sarah Charley, taught Arnold about the plants. Like all good Navajos, he started the plants related to sheep; the toxic ones, the beneficial ones, the ones for dyeing wool.

Charley was a renowned medicine woman, herbalist and weaver. After school, Arnold would follow the tinkling bells of her flock high into the Carrizo Mountains.

"Arnold just kinda tagged along with her everywhere," his mother Lena Charley Clifford says.

Together, they gathered plants and brewed them into rich browns, yellows and greens. For crimson, they harvested the fat, red aphids that live on the oblong pads of the prickly pear cactus (*Oppuntia*).

"I heard a story about a plant once and that was it," Arnold says. The ability to remember things without writing them down, is called 'the Navajo mind.'

Charley taught him practical uses for plants: how to make diapers from the satiny inner bark of Cliffrose. How to make sandals from Bailey's yucca. How to make structures with willow. As Arnold grew, she taught him the medicinal plants.

Then, he learned the ceremonial plants; their sacred names and chants. She taught him rituals and prayers passed through generations of shamans, herbalists, stargazers and hand tremblers in their family.

Burdened and blessed with this knowledge, Arnold struggles to save his culture. He's always trying to teach the old ways to young Navajos, whether they are listening or not.

When Sarah Charley died in 2002, she broke the Navajo tradition of matrilineal inheritance, leaving her sheep and ancestral lands to Arnold. Soon after, he discovered a low-growing buckwheat and named it after her. It is found on a single, windswept mesa near the border of Arizona and New Mexico.

❧

Two years later, I'm standing on that mesa with my mother and Arnold. He stares across the desert, wearing jeans and a flannel. My mom and I are bundled against the knife-sharp wind. At our feet, a tuft of burnt yellow clings to the steep, ferrous cliffside. *"Eriogonum Sarahaie,"* Arnold says, in his rhythmic lilt. "Sarah's buckwheat."

Like all the women in my family, my mom is a plants-woman. She kneels down and touches the delicate petals. Her hat flops in her face. Soon we are on our bellies in the dirt, laughing. We are like sisters. She is beautiful beyond anything I can remember.

This family-plant connection solidified Arnold's interest in me. My great-grandmother was a botanical explorer in the early 1900s. A tough, small Quaker woman, she helped map northeastern British Columbia, and crossed rivers on horseback. Near the Peace River, there is a mountain named for her. She discovered many plants that are now ordinary. Her home and garden, outside Philadelphia, is now a starving non-profit dedicated to preserving native North American plants.

Driving back to Beclabito, my mom takes the wheel. She zooms across the roadless sagebrush. With her back as straight as a board, she's every bit a proper Philadelphia woman, even on the Rez.

The sun sets. The desert turns violet. And the cool hush of dusk settles in the car. After a while Arnold says, "I think some people are just meant to find things. Maybe the Holy People see how dedicated you are to your science, how long you've been out there. So they push something toward you, a new species. That's the Navajo teaching."

But below the soil where these rare plants cling to life, lie resources sought by interests more powerful than a lone Navajo scientist. Precious reserves of natural gas, oil, uranium and coal snake underfoot. Throughout the Reservation, bulldozers prepare the way for miners and drillers seeking these non-botanical treasures.

It's a hot, clear day in July. The summer monsoons are still a mirage. Arnold and I cruise east from Shiprock. We pass the Four Corners Power Plant and Navajo Mine. We drive until the road becomes a narrow thread that disappears into the Badlands. I step out onto the baked, gray moonscape. It crunches underfoot. A blue dome yawns overhead. We walk in the heat.

I'm respectably dressed for a woman in Navajoland—jeans and a long-sleeved shirt. It's over a hundred degrees out. And I'm hot as hell.

We wander through a maze of hollow, gray hills strewn with petrified logs. We find bones as long as I am tall, shattered and encrusted at our feet. Arnold picks a spot and sits down. "I think you'll like this," he says.

Soon we are on our bellies in the dirt. Arnold is telling old Navajo stories while we sift through a mound of fossils. I hold up a rock and he says, "That's ancient turtle shell." Or, "That's bone." Or, "That's a shark's tooth." I touch the secrets of the earth. And he decodes them for me.

"Each landform has a sacred story," Arnold says. "The stories remind us how to live. They tell of how to avoid hardships. If you don't live right, you tend to have hardships, you know."

Arnold points to an outcropping streaked with coal. "The mine's expanding illegally," he says. "They've already chased off the landowners."

I wonder what my own personal fossil record will look like. And I scramble to think of sacred landforms in my life.

A few weeks later, I get a call from Arnold. "Remember that place we went with all those fossils?" he says. "It's gone. Bulldozed."

It's 3:00 A.M. when I pull into Shiprock. The town is a glowing sprawl of tents and rodeos and carnival rides. The Shiprock Fair outshines even the neon fast food signs on the main drag. I troll the acres of dirt parking lot. On the far edge, I find the Yei Bi Chei ceremony.

My car thermometer reads 12 degrees. I don every layer I have and follow a line of Port-o-potties to the ceremony. A thousand Navajos huddle around fires of juniper, cedar and pinyon. Plumes of aromatic smoke unfurl into the night.

The fires mark a long, dirt stage that leads to a Hogan. Inside, medicine men chant and drum. Outside, generators rev and thrum. The stage is lit. A collective breath is held.

Wearing jeans and a ratty down jacket, I'm hoping to blend in, knowing I won't. Some Navajos stare at me. Others ignore me. I scan the fire-lit faces for Arnold.

The dancers file out. They wear blue masks, decorated hides and feathered headdresses. Their bodies are painted white. They bend low and shake their rattles in unison. They stamp their feet, tip their masks skyward and whoop at the stars.

Across the fire, Arnold's face materializes, as if he's been there the whole time. He's trained on the dancers, his lips moving to the words of the songs. I make my way through the crowd and gush when I find him. He gives me a quick hug and pushes me toward the fire. "Stay warm," he says, then disappears.

An impenetrable knot of Navajos circles the fire. Elderly women draped in blankets, are slumped closest to the heat. I patrol the outside, soaking up the meager warmth.

"Hey!" someone yells. I know they're talking to me. I look up. A Navajo guy with long black hair is staring at me. He can't be more than 20. "Is this your first time?" he says, staggering over to me.

"It is," I say.

He leans in close, eyes wide. "Those are our gods," he says. "Our GODS." Alcohol floats on his breath. Together, we stare at the dancers. "You've never seen anything like it have you?" he says.

"No," I say.

"I can tell you're enjoying it," he says, smirking at me. His friends gather around, egging him on. I back away into the darkness. An announcer squawks over the loudspeaker in Navajo.

When Arnold appears, I ask for a translation. "He says there have been complaints about white people in our midst."

I'm mortified.

"He also says that we have allowed white people to observe the Yei Bi Chei, since the beginning. The ceremony blesses all who witness it."

The sky lightens from black to blue. "This is the last dance," Arnold says. "I'll catch up with you after."

An old Navajo man with a deeply creased face and a cowboy hat approaches me. "Do you have any corn pollen?"

"No," I say.

He hands me a small plastic bag filled with yellow dust. "Rub it on the dancers when they go by, and say a prayer."

The crowd gets to their feet and readies their pollen. The dancers bolt. The crowd converges on them. I rub pollen on one of the dancers and say a prayer. En masse, the crowd stops. One by one, the dancers walk to the horizon. They face east and make praying motions. Light spills across the desert, obliterating their figures.

I stare at the sunrise for a long time. When I turn around, the crowd has scattered. A few Navajos linger around smoldering fires. Starlings hop from one discarded corncob to another. Ravens pick at trash. The fairground looks a dusty warzone.

❧

PEOPLE FILL THE HALLS OF my great-grandmother's house. They've come to hear Arnold's lecture on desert plants.

But Arnold isn't here. I should have budgeted for Navajo time. Minutes before his lecture starts, I get a text. "Not gonna make it. Still in Tennessee."

My stomach flips into my throat. I throw together some photos from our last trip, rig the projector and stand to face a roomful of botanists.

I am not a scientist. But I know what I have to do. This is my worst fear. My great-grandmother peers at me from a portrait on the back wall. I take a deep breath, as if through a tiny straw, and dive into my botanical adventures with Arnold.

Arnold's voice is clear in my head. As I flip through photographs, everything he's taught me pours out—plant names, uses, geology, cultural history.

The audience leans forward. I never met my great-grandmother, but I imagine she's listening. My mother and aunt are sitting in the back of the room. This is my tribe.

·•·

THE FOLLOWING AFTERNOON, ARNOLD pulls up in his red pickup. Two Navajo women, rumpled from the long drive, hop out. He introduces me to his girlfriend and her sister.

His girlfriend is gorgeous, tall with long, shiny black hair and proud features. My jaw hinges shut and my cheeks heat up. I shake her hand and smile. Inside, I am crushed.

Arnold and I have never kissed. We've never held hands. But I had agonized over his question for the past three years. At the time, I wanted a mentor, not a lover. I thought my romantic feelings might grow in that gray area. The deadline had long come and gone and I had said nothing.

That day at the pizza place in Durango, I knew the answer to Arnold's question. I just didn't want to lose him. In the end, I lost him anyways. We've never spoken since that trip to Philadelphia. But what he showed me was more valuable than any romantic relationship. I didn't need to be a part of his tribe. I had my own. ⤳

Author Biographies

Kendra Atleework was born and raised in the high desert of Owens Valley, below the Eastern Sierra Nevada mountains. Her writing has appeared in *Best American Essays 2015* and elsewhere. She received an MFA in creative writing from the University of Minnesota in 2016 and hold a BA from Scripps College. Her literary essays about Owens Valley and water politics have appeared in *Guernica*, *Hayden's Ferry Review* and *The Morning News*, among others. Atleework won the 2014 AWP Intro Journals Award in nonfiction. She has taught creative writing at the University of Minnesota and is on the board of directors of the Ellen Meloy Fund for Desert Writers. Her memoir, *Sweetwater: Life and Change in the Rain Shadow of the Sierra Nevada,* maps the convergence of family, place, and history, and is forthcoming in spring of 2020 from Algonquin Books.

Nathaniel Brodie has worked as a backcountry wilderness ranger, dry-laid stone mason, farmer, carpenter, beekeeper, journalist, troutslayer, and editor. He received a Master of Fine Arts Degree in Nonfiction Creative Writing from the University of Arizona. He was the recipient of the PEN Northwest Margery Davis Boyden Wilderness Writing Residency. He is the author of *Steel on Stone: Living and Working in the Grand Canyon* (Trinity University Press, 2019) and the coeditor of Forest *Under Story: Creative Inquiry in an Old-Growth Forest* (University of Washington Press, 2015). He lives with his wife and daughter in Portland, Oregon.

Tara FitzGerald holds a BA in English Language and Literature from Oxford University in the UK. Fitzgerald's nonfiction writing has appeared in *Guernica*, *Vela* and *The Common*, among others. She has completed residencies at Art Farm and the Kimmel Nelson Harding Center for the Arts. Fitzgerald was based in Mexico City for six years as a freelance reporter, writing for publications including *Monocle, Wallpaper, Esquire*

Latin America. Food and Wine and *Departures* magazine. Prior to her work in Mexico, she was a staff writer for Reuters news agency, based in the United Kingdom, Germany, the United Arab Emirates and Russia.

Kenneth Garcia is the Associate Director, Institute for Scholarship in the Liberal Arts, at the University of Notre Dame. He received his PhD in Theology from the University of Notre Dame in 2008. His academic writings include a book which won an award for "Best Book Published in Theology in 2012," and scholarly essays in The Journal of Academic Freedom, Theological Studies and Horizons. More recently, Garcia has turned to literary nonfiction and has been published in *The Gettysburg Review, The Southwest Review, Saint Katherine Review, Notre Dame Magazine* and *Hunger Mountain.* His book, *Pilgrim River: A Spiritual Memoir,* was published by Angelico Press in 2018.

Summer Hess manages Sage Step Designs in Wenatchee, Washington, offering editorial and creative services. She serves as managing editor for Out There Outdoors, the Inland Northwest's guide to travel, adventure, and outdoor living. Her work has appeared in *Field & Compass, Nspire Magazine, The Spinoff* (New Zealand), and in a forthcoming book chapter published by Across the Disciplines called *Visual Thinking Strategies in the Composition Classroom.* Hess earned an MFA in non-fiction writing from Eastern Washington University. She worked in San Pedro de Atacama, Chile (2006) through a Chilean Ministry of Education teaching program and returned through a Student Fulbright Award (2011) to research the history of travel and tourism.

Charles Hood has spent his career working and living in the Mojave Desert. A selection of his desert-centered work earned him the 2016 Felix Pollak Prize in poetry, and in March 2017 Wisconsin University Press released the contest-winning manuscript, *Partially Excited States.* He also wrote *Mouth,* 2016 winner of the Kenneth Patchen Innovative Novel Prize. Hood's book *South × South* was the 2013 Hollis Summers Prize winner, a book that recounts his experiences in Antarctica as an artist-in-residence with the National Science Foundation.

Maya Kapoor graduated in 2015 with an MFA in creative writing from the University of Arizona. Kapoor has more than a decade's experience as a field biologist and environmental educator in the Western United States and Latin America and holds a master's in biology from Arizona State University. She serves as associate editor for *High Country News'* southern coverage area from Davis, California. She also writes about science, environmental policy and social justice. Kapoor's writing has been published in *An Essay Daily Reader* (Coffee House Press); *The Sonoran Desert: A Literary Field Guide* (University of Arizona Press); *ISLE: Interdisciplinary Studies in Literature and Environment; Edible Baja Arizona;* and Terrain.org.

Michael Kula has an eclectic background which includes coursework in six foreign languages. His current position is in Interdisciplinary Arts and Sciences at the University of Washington, Tacoma, where he is an Associate Professor of Creative Writing. His writing has focused on both creative nonfiction and historical fiction, and for it he has received awards from the Pacific Northwest Writers Association and the US National Parks Service, which selected him as Writer-in-Residence for the Homestead National Monument. Kula has published more than a dozen essays and short stories, as well as a novel, *The Good Doctor,* which was released by a publisher that specializes in books that are "rooted in the land" and seek to "capture the physical places we inhabit." For his proposed project, he conducted fieldwork in the Namib and Kalahari deserts of southern Africa.

Rebecca Lawton is the Executive Director of PLAYA, an artists' and scientists' residency program in Summer Lake, Oregon. She is an author, instructor, and fluvial geologist whose work explores wild and human nature. Lawton's winning 2015 proposal is now a chapter in her book, *The*

Oasis This Time: Living and Dying With Water in the West, released 2019 by Torrey Press. An early woman guide on Western whitewater, Rebecca rowed the Colorado in Grand Canyon and other wilderness rivers for 14 seasons. Her work as a scientist has focused on ancient and modern ephemeral streams, the movement of sediment, and water turbidity levels that affect fish growth and survival. Her writing honors include a 2014 Fulbright Visiting Research Chair Award, a 2014 WILLA Award for original softcover fiction, the 2006 Ellen Meloy Fund Award for Desert Writers, and several residencies.

Lawrence Lenhart studied writing at the University of Pittsburgh and holds an MFA from the University of Arizona. His first collection of essays is *The Well-Stocked and Gilded Cage* (Outpost19). Recent writing appears in *Conjunctions, Creative Nonfiction, Fourth Genre, Passages North,* and *Prairie Schooner.* He is a professor of fiction and nonfiction at Northern Arizona University and a reviews editor and assistant fiction editor of *DIAGRAM*.

Kimberly Meyer holds a doctoral degree in Literature and Creative Writing from the University of Houston, where she was the recipient of several fellowships and grants. Her essays have appeared widely in magazines and journals and have been anthologized in the *Best American Travel Writing.* She teaches literature courses in the Great Books at the University of Houston, and lives in that thriving, multicultural city of no zoning with her husband and daughters. Funded by a Houston Arts Alliance Established Artist Grant, she and her eldest daughter retraced the footsteps of Felix Fabri, a medieval Dominican friar whose written account of his travels resonated with Meyer, the summer after the Arab Spring. Those intertwined pilgrimages—his and hers—became the basis for *The Book of Wanderings: A Mother-Daughter Pilgrimage,* written in part during a month-long Full Residency Fellowship at the Vermont Studio Center, and published in 2015 by Little, Brown.

Patrick Mondaca served in Baghdad, Iraq with the U.S. Army and as a security advisor for a humanitarian organization in South Darfur, Sudan. He earned an MS in Global Affairs from New York University and an MFA in Creative Writing from Fairleigh Dickinson University. Currently he is a researcher, writer, and adjunct professor at John Jay College of Criminal Justice. Mondaca's work has appeared in *The Washington Post, The Globe and Mail, USA Today, The Hill,* and *U.S. News & World Report,* among others. Mondaca lives in Montclair, New Jersey with his wife and daughter.

Naseem Rakha is a geologist, educator, speaker, and award winning author and journalist whose novel, *The Crying Tree,* has earned international acclaim for its frank examination of crime, punishment, sexual identity and forgiveness. Rakha's commentaries can be found in *The Guardian* and she was a contributor to National Public Radio. When not writing, Rakha spends her time hiking, climbing, rafting and photographing areas throughout the American West. Her work can also be found in the *Los Angeles Review* and *Gold Man Review.* Rakha is currently working on a new novel. She lives in Oregon with her husband and son, dog, cats and snake.

Caroline Treadway is a writer and photographer based in Boulder, Colorado. Her words and images appear in magazines, books and newspapers worldwide. Her advertising clients include New Balance and National Geographic Online. A native of Washington D.C., Caroline attended the Potomac School. In 2000, she graduated magna cum laude from Manhattanville College in Purchase, N.Y., with a Bachelor's degree in World Religion. Caroline graduated in 2010 from Boston University with a Master's Degree in Journalism.

Kathryn Wilder has lived in and written about each of the Four Corners states, focusing on aridity, water, and the details of place as she worked on desert rivers and ranches, learning firsthand the fragility of these desert ecosystems. Wilder's work has appeared in many publications and a dozen anthologies. In 2016 Wilder was Artist-in-Residence at Denali National Park and Preserve, and a finalist for the Ellen Meloy Fund Desert Writers Award. She is a 2017 graduate of the low-residency MFA program at the Institute of American Indian Arts in Santa Fe. Wilder lives in Dolores, Colorado.

Diana Woodcock has lived for more than a decade on the Arabian Desert's edge where, since receiving an MFA in Creative Writing in 2004, she has been teaching creative writing, environmental literature and composition at Virginia Commonwealth University in Qatar. In 2011, she received the Distinguished Achievements in Research Award from her university. She has received four research grants from her university to study endangered desert and wetland ecosystems. Woodcock's fourth book, about endangered plants of the Arabian Desert, is due out in 2019. She is the author of three full-length collections of poetry: *Tread Softly, Under the Spell of a Persian Nightingale;* and *Swaying on the Elephant's Shoulders,* and seven chapbooks. Woodcock's work has also appeared in numerous journals and anthologies. Woodcock is based in Midlothian, Virginia.

Thank You Valued Donors!

Waterston Desert Writing Prize Donors for Fiscal Year 2018 – 2019

Oregon Community Foundation

The Waterston Desert Writing Prize endowment is managed by the Oregon Community Foundation. The endowment was established by actor Sam Waterston, after whom the prize is named. As the endowment for the prize grows, so will the annual prize amount.

Deschutes Cultural Coalition

The Prize is supported by a grant from the Deschutes Cultural Coalition with funds from the Oregon Cultural Trust to support Oregon's arts, heritage, and the humanities.

Great Basin

High Desert Museum
PLAYA

Mojave

Becker Capital Management
Julia Kennedy Cochran
The Helen Foundation
Gail and Ronald Hill
Charles McGrath
The Roundhouse Foundation
Trish and William Smith
Starview Foundation
Ellen Waterston
Waterston Family Foundation
Writing Ranch

Kalahari

Deschutes County Arts & Culture
    Grant Program
Deschutes Cultural Coalition
Louise Hawker
Les Joslin
Timothy Lester
Dick and Suzie Linford
Watermark Communications

Sahara

Anonymous Donor
James Anderson
Randall Barna
Bowtie Catering
Jennifer Delahunty
Ted Haynes
Sue and Michael Hollern
Bruce Jackson
William Kinsey
Joan Kinsey
Kathy Lawrence
Jacqueline Thea
Jeff Tryens

Sonoran

Jim Cornelius
Dixie Eckford
Cheri Helfenstein
Karen Stanard
Suzanne Staples
Lorraine Stuart
Helen Vandervort

Note: This list is current as of June 1, 2019. Please let us know about any inadvertent omissions.